M000220794

Effective Leadership Habits

Effective Leadership Habits

A Concise Guide from an Islamic Perspective

Muhammad Bashir Agboola

Revised and Updated Edition

Dedication

This humble effort is dedicated to my loving family – particularly my wife and kids, whose understanding and support, by God's permission, has made it possible.

Table of Contents

Introduction

This book is a guide to aid anyone looking to develop and/or improve their leadership skills. It is presented in a concise format to enable quick comprehension of important leadership principles and some key leadership habits and practices of highly effective leaders. It draws on universal leadership principles as taught in Islam and is applicable to anyone, Muslims and non-Muslims alike, looking to become better leaders.

Islam teaches that God-consciousness should pervade all aspects of human life and should not be limited to religious rituals alone. Thus, leading ethically, and striving to excel in one's role as a leader is considered a religious duty for any Muslim leader.

This book draws on Islamic principles as taught in the Qur'an and Sunnah (sayings and practices of the prophet of Islam, Muhammad, peace be upon him), and on examples of effective leadership practices as demonstrated by the Prophet and his successors (Caliphs). These same values are observable in effective, ethical leaders of various faiths and traditions, making these principles truly universal.

The book is inspired by the author's own experience as a leader and C-suite executive in corporate America, as well as his extensive study of management and leadership principles from both the Islamic and Western traditions. It is the author's hope that it brings benefit to a varied audience looking for guidance on universal and everlasting principles of ethical and effective leadership.

Note on Arabic words, Translations and cited Islamic Works

Arabic terms are translated in most instances in the book. In a few cases, the transliteration of an Arabic term is also included to maintain as close a tie to its original Arabic word as possible. The words *Allah* and *God* are used interchangeably throughout the book. Additionally, the names of referenced chapters in the Qur'an (Islam's Holy text) are cited along with the chapter and verse numbers, (e.g. Al-Anbiyah 21:73, refers to Surat Al-Anbiyah (Chapter of the Prophets/ Chapter 21, Verse 73 of the Qur'an). The referenced verses are also presented in both the original Arabic text and the English translation of the meaning.

It is customary in Islamic tradition when referencing the Prophets of God to add a salutary prayer after their names. Hence, the statement, **Sallallahu alayhi wa sallam** (abbreviated in this book as **saw**), which means *peace be upon him*, is repeated after the name of Prophet Muhammad (saw) in the following pages.

Finally, there are extensive references to the sayings (Hadith/pl. Ahadith) of Prophet Muhammad (saw), throughout the book. These references are from classical authoritative works of Hadith, including Sahih Al-Bukhari, Sahih Muslim, Sunan Ibn Majah, Abu Dawud, and others. The Hadith work or works from which a particular saying is quoted is listed after the respective hadith.

Chapter 1: What is Leadership?

There are many definitions of leadership. A common theme present in most of those definitions is the idea of an individual (the leader) exerting influence over others (a group or groups) towards the achievement of some common goals or purpose.

Islam views leadership as a trust (*amanah*) conferred on an individual by those he or she leads; a trust that he will guide them, protect their interests, and exert himself in bringing benefit to them while averting any undesirable outcomes from them. This fundamentally describes the nature of leadership, irrespective of the context. There is another critical dimension to the concept of leadership as taught in Islam, which is that not only is the leader accountable to the people he or she leads and who have entrusted him with their affairs, he is also (and most importantly) accountable to God for his actions and for the sincerity of his efforts in the discharge of his duties. The trust then is conferred on the leader by God, and by the people he serves.

Leadership involves exerting influence over the efforts of others, who entrust the leader with the protection of their interests and their welfare, and the accomplishment of the group's goals. This trust is a divine responsibility, the discharge of which should be considered with seriousness. There is a grave warning against negligence in this respect. The Prophet (saw) said, "*Verily, you may earnestly desire a position of leadership, but you will regret it on the Day of Resurrection*." - Sahih Al-Bukhari

Hence from an Islamic perspective, leadership effectiveness can be thought of in terms of the degree to which the constituents' interests and goals are met, the means via which those outcomes were pursued and achieved, and the degree to which the actions and intentions of the leader reflect the consciousness of his or her accountability to God in the discharge of their duties.

It therefore behooves a leader to strive to improve his or her leadership skills, and to strive to be the best leader that they can be. Prophet Muhammad (saw) said: "*Verily, Allah has prescribed excellence in everything.*" - Sahih Muslim.

He also said: "*Seeking knowledge is an obligation upon every Muslim* " -Sunan Ibn Majah

Thus, a leader should pursue leadership excellence, and seek to improve his or her skills by acquiring knowledge on how to lead effectively, including seeking out and learning from the examples of successful leaders.

It is not uncommon for someone to feel ill-prepared or unqualified for leadership, and to shy away from leadership responsibilities. Humility and a strong sense of accountability often cause some of the most qualified people to shy away from leadership positions. Even the most accomplished leaders can be afflicted with the so-called "impostor syndrome" where they experience phycological doubts about their own qualifications and accomplishments and harbor fears of being found to be "frauds". Focusing on educating oneself on leadership principles and practicing the habits we shall discuss in this book can be helpful in dealing with these phycological barriers, particularly for new leaders.

Nonetheless, it is important to have enough self-awareness of ones capabilities, and to seek to improve oneself in areas where one is deficient in leadership qualities. Indeed, effective leadership principles can be taught but the leader still must have the interest and capability to put those principles to work. Hence the earlier warning that many people who assume positions of leadership will in the end be regretful and would have been better off not taking those positions.

This is illustrated by an incident involving Abu Dharr, a companion of Prophet Muhammad (saw), who reported the response he got upon asking for a leadership position. "*O Abu Dharr*", the Prophet said to him, "*you are weak, and it is a position of public trust.*

Verily, on the Day of Resurrection it will only result in regret, **except for one who takes it by right and fulfills its duties***.*" In another narration of this incident, the Prophet said to Abu Dharr, "*I love for you what I love for myself. Do not command even two people, and do not manage the property of an orphan*." - Sahih Muslim. We see herein the advice given to Abu Dharr, an upright and pious man, who nonetheless, the Prophet deemed ill-suited for leadership positions.

Thus, a person should not permit self-doubt to discourage him from serving and should instead strive to improve his leadership skills through seeking knowledge, mentorship, coaching, and practice. He should nonetheless try to be objective about his capabilities and be constantly mindful of his accountability to both his creator and his constituents.

Types of leadership

Leadership can be formal or informal, and both of those can be within various spheres of life, e.g. political, professional, military, social, religious, et cetera.

Formal leadership is backed by structures and processes that lead to the emergence of the leader and confer him or her with the authority with which they lead. Most discussions on leadership tend to focus on this type of leadership, be it in business or political contexts.

Informal leadership on the other hand is not derived from formal authority but can be best thought of as exerting influence without the formal authority to do so (that is, leadership with implied authority). This is the realm within which many people exert leadership, and the broader sense in which everybody can be considered a leader.

Islam recognizes that leaders exists in multiple contexts, not just in the context of formal organizational structures. Hence Prophet Muhammad (saw) said: "*Each one of you is a shepherd, and each one of you will be questioned about how he managed his flock*" – Sahih Al-Bukhari/Sahih Muslim.

The simile of the leader as a shepherd is excellent for describing the relationship between the leader and those he serves. This simile is applicable to leadership in a general context, whether in corporate and political settings, or in the context of a religious organization. A good shepherd tends to his flock, directing them to where to graze, and watches over them while they do so. He carries the young or injured member of his flock and guides the flock back home safely at the end of the day, all the while tolerating various hardships and inconveniences the role entails. So must a good leader guide those he serves towards the attainment of the group's objectives, advocate for and ensure fair dealings amongst them, and protect the group from internal and external threats.

The statement that everyone is a shepherd implies that everyone has some leadership responsibility within their sphere of influence. For example, a husband and wife are both leaders within the context of the family, just as a manager, elected official, or a member of the clergy are leaders within their own respective groups. Each one will likewise be ultimately held accountable for the performance of their leadership duties by their creator.

Leadership Role Models

One of the best ways to learn a skill is to emulate the successful practitioners of that skill. This allows for learning from the example and experience of successful practitioners, noting what works from their practice, as well as learning from their failures. This philosophy applies to leadership as well.

Learning the right lessons about leadership from and following the examples of effective leaders are means of honing one's leadership qualities. Great leaders often cite other influential people as their role models and inspiration. Throughout written history, studying the life and performance of successful leaders has proven to be one of the most effective paths to leadership development.

The ultimate examples of leaders are the Prophets (peace be upon them all). While we often talk about and think of the Prophets mainly as spiritual figures whose purposes were to minister to their communities, their lives, as chronicled in the Qur'an and other Abrahamic scriptures, illustrate the highest levels of leadership and sacrifice from which modern day leaders can draw inspiration.

While the lives and times of these great leaders were different and their leadership challenges varied, we see common threads in their situations. They were massive change agents who sought to influence society and effect radical change, while almost always being without any political or military authority. They often had to work against established power structures and ingrained habits and beliefs. They faced covert and overt opposition, including threats of brutal violence to themselves and their followers. They experienced success and failures in their missions and demonstrated the utmost example of nobility in dealing with both their successes and their adversities.

If we assess leadership effectiveness by the extent of the leader's influence on people over time, we cannot but agree that there has been no greater influence on humanity than that of the Prophets as judged by their lasting legacies and the continued adherence to the faiths, principles, and ideas that they propagated. It therefore makes a lot of sense for leaders to learn about the qualities that made these people very influential and effective, and to draw inspiration and guidance from their noble and wise qualities.

We see several references to this in the Qur'an, where Allah states regarding the Prophets:

وَجَعَلْنَا مِنْهُمْ أَئِمَّةً يَهْدُونَ بِأَمْرِنَا لَمَّا صَبَرُوا وَكَانُوا بِآيَاتِنَا يُوقِنُونَ (32:24)

And We appointed, from among them, leaders, giving guidance under Our command, so long as they persevered with patience and continued to have faith in Our Signs. – Sajdah 32:24

وَجَعَلْنَاهُمْ أَئِمَّةً يَهْدُونَ بِأَمْرِنَا وَأَوْحَيْنَا إِلَيْهِمْ فِعْلَ الْخَيْرَاتِ وَإِقَامَ الصَّلَاةِ وَإِيتَاء الزَّكَاةِ وَكَانُوا لَنَا عَابِدِينَ (21:73)

And We made them leaders, guiding (men) by Our Command, and We sent them inspiration to do good

11

deeds, to establish regular prayers, and to practice regular charity; and they constantly served Us (and Us only). - Al- Anbiyah 21:73

لَقَدْ كَانَ لَكُمْ فِي رَسُولِ اللَّهِ أُسْوَةٌ حَسَنَةٌ لِّمَن كَانَ يَرْجُو اللَّهَ وَالْيَوْمَ الْآخِرَ وَذَكَرَ اللَّهَ كَثِيرًا (33:21)

VERILY, in the Apostle of God you have a good example for everyone who looks forward [with hope and awe] to God and the Last Day and remembers God unceasingly. – Ahzab 33:21

Narrations about the lives of the Prophets abound in the Qur'an and in the Sunnah (sayings and practices) of Prophet Muhammad (saw). In those narrations, we learn of the various beautiful qualities exemplified by the Prophets, and how they related with the people they were sent to. For example, we learn about the patience of Ayyub (Job) in coping with personal adversity in the form of a debilitating illness; of the resilience and perseverance of Noah in his unsuccessful effort at ministering to his recalcitrant people; and of the strong faith and conviction of Yusuf (Joseph) in the face of treachery, injustice, and temptation. We also learn of the courage and leadership of Musa (Moses) in freeing his people from the oppression and bondage of Fir'aun (Pharaoh) and his Egyptian forces.

A study of the life of Prophet Muhammad (saw) reveals a treasure trove of leadership wisdom, gleaned from his role as a spiritual leader, a statesman, a family man, a businessman, a military leader, and a humanitarian. Historians and scholars of leadership studies have studied his life extensively and commended him for his leadership mastery. Included amongst them are non-Muslim scholars such as George Bernard Shaw, and the world's foremost professor of Leadership studies, John Adair. Additionally, Michael H. Hart ranked Prophet Muhammed (saw) at the top of the list in his book, *The 100: A Ranking of the Most Influential Persons in History*. Hart ranked Prophet Muhammad (saw) over other historical figures, including Jesus and Moses, because his analysis showed that Muhammad (saw) was supremely successful in both secular and religious terms.

We also see excellent examples of leadership at work in the lives of many of the prominent figures in Islam, in particular, the four *Rightly Guided Successors* (Khulafah Ar-Rashedun)/Caliphs of Prophet Muhammad (saw). These were the people who led the Muslim world, in succession, after the death of the Prophet (saw). Amongst these distinguish individuals, perhaps none demonstrated the best leadership qualities better than the second caliph, Umar Ibn Khattab. He was, like many of the other companions of Prophet Muhammad (saw), reputed for his piety, humility, ascetism, and a strong sense of justice and fairness. Less appreciated today however is his leadership and administrative genius. It was under his leadership that Islam witnessed a major expansion into lands hitherto occupied by the Byzantine and Persian empires, Jerusalem came under the control of the Muslims (and remained so for the next 500 hundred years), and many fiscal, judicial, and administrative structures of the Islamic state were implemented. These included the creation of a pension plan for military members and the family of the Prophet (saw), as well as the creation of the Islamic Judicial system with the appointment of the first provincial judges to Basrah and Kufah (in modern day Iraq).

Like the Prophet (saw) and Abu Bakr before him, Umar was a firm believer in "Management by Walking Around", often moving around the capital city of Madinah incognito at night to assess the condition of the people, and to render direct aid to them. He appointed the best qualified people to official positions and held his leadership team accountable for the discharge of their duties.

Another example of a great leadership role model can be seen in the case of Caliph Ali, the fourth successor and cousin of Prophet Muhammad (saw). Amongst his noble qualities is his immense wisdom and intellect. His many epistles on a variety of topics including philosophy, faith, leadership and administration remain a source of inspiration today, as they have been throughout Islamic history. One such work is his letter to Malik Al-Ashtar, whom he appointed as the governor of Egypt. A translation of the letter is included as an appendix in this book, and excerpts from the letter are referenced throughout the book. One such passage from the letter is shown below wherein Caliph Ali advised Malik Al-Ashtar on the need to study good leadership and management principles using positive role models:

"It is imperative on you to study carefully the principles which have inspired just and good rulers who have gone before you. Give close thought to the example of our prophet, his traditions, and the commandments of the Holy Qur'an and whatever you might have assimilated from my own way of dealing with things."

Another example of the spirit of leadership in Islam and of some of the habits discussed in this book is reflected in the inaugural address of Caliph Abu Bakr. Addressing the people assembled for prayer after his selection as the new khalifah/Caliph, he said:

"O people, I have been put in authority over you and I am not the best of you. If I do the right thing, then help me. If I do wrong, then correct me. Truthfulness is a sacred trust and lying is a betrayal. The weak among you

is strong in my sight. I will surely try to remove their pain and suffering. And the strong among you is weak to me. I will, if Allah wills, fulfill the rights in full. When obscene things spread among any nation, calamities continue to descend upon them. As long as I obey Allah and His messenger, you should obey me. If I do not obey Allah and His messenger, then obedience to me is not an obligation upon you. Now, stand for the prayer, may Allah have mercy upon you." - Al-Sirah al-Nabawiyah

Thus, leadership development in the Islamic tradition includes studying the examples of the great leaders of the past, particularly the prophets, as well as the men and women, past and present, who have demonstrated some of the same noble leadership qualities. Studying their lives, leadership styles and habits, and emulating them in those qualities that enabled them to lead effectively, are great ways to become highly effective as leaders in whatever context we are charged to lead.

Chapter 2: Effective Leadership Habits

There are various habits and qualities that leaders must exhibit in order to lead effectively. While these would vary in form and relative importance depending on leadership context (i.e. form of leadership, organizational entity, community, time, and place), certain practices, or habits are very fundamental and are critical to leadership effectiveness and success. As mentioned earlier, there are various examples from the Qur'an and the Sunnah and from the lives and examples of effective leaders in history and contemporary times that point to the importance of these practices in leadership effectiveness. We have identified and explained the most important of these practices in the following pages.

It is worth emphasizing however that these habits are not the only important ones that leaders need to develop, but rather, they are the foundation upon which effective leadership practices are built. These are also not limited to leadership within any particular organizational context, but rather, they are equally important in various aspects of life, including political, professional, social, and religious settings.

We also describe them as habits since they are things one must do on a continuous basis in order to gain the benefits associated with them. They are not time-bound tasks that are done once and forgotten. To become habits, these practices must become so much a routine, to the point that they become subconscious, meaning that one continues doing them until they become a natural part of one's character and are not perceived as forced or contrived.

Like many of the most beneficial things in life, these practices are not strange or esoteric. Rather, they are commonsense yet uncommon practices that, while relatively easy to learn and understand, many leaders find challenging to practice consistently.

These habits of highly effective leaders discussed in this book are:

1. Having Sincerity of Purpose
2. Being Servant Leaders
3. Leading with Integrity
4. Communicating with Impact
5. Dealing Justly with All
6. Developing and Maintaining Trust
7. Engaging in Participative Leadership
8. Possessing and Projecting a Positive Attitude
9. Understanding Balance and Relative Priorities
10. Leading with Empathy
11. Practicing Self-Care

In the following chapters, we will discuss these habits and explain the benefits associated with developing and consistently practicing them.

Chapter 3: Having Sincerity of Purpose

Human actions are spurned by some motivation or purpose, irrespective of whether that purpose is deemed logical, beneficial, or otherwise, and whether or not that purpose is well articulated or understood. People are generally driven to action by motivations, which at its barest, could be to avoid pain, or to make gain. The enthusiasm, passion, and energy with which they pursue whatever goal they are working towards is largely influenced by the degree of dedication to the purpose they pursue and their conviction in its merit or benefit.

Leadership is an exercise in influence exertion towards the achievement of some common goals, and the leader's efforts are greatly influenced by his motivations and commitment towards the group's goals. Thus, the most fundamental of the effective leadership habits is that of sincerity of purpose. A leader must serve a cause higher than his own self-interest. His purpose in leadership should be to fulfil the requirements of that position and to achieve the goals of the commonality (whether the constituents be shareholders, employees, citizens, or members of a religious organization). This sincerity of purpose, or intentionality, allows for a strong commitment to purpose, and the alignment of the leader's vision with the shared purpose.

The Prophet (saw) explained that actions are judged based on the intention with which they are performed: *"(The value of) an action depends on the intention behind it. A man will be rewarded only for what he intended"* – Sahih Al-Bukhari/Sahih Muslim

Hence, for one's actions to be acceptable, they must meet the criteria of sincerity of purpose and conformity of the actions with the goals and values of the group (and importantly for Muslims, with Islamic ethical values). Thus, a lofty intention is a necessary but insufficient condition for the acceptance of a deed. A sincere intention needs to be coupled with lawful and ethical action. This is both in the context of performing religious worship as well as in carrying out secular duties. Man's action should have behind it a purpose that isn't capricious, even as he is entitled to seek for himself fair benefits accruing from his fulfilling his duties. Much of the failure in leadership we have witnessed historically in the world can be linked to the leader's lack of sincere commitment to the group's mission and values, which then causes the leader to act in ways that are detrimental to the group's interests, and or selfishly advantageous to himself and his supporters. Often, a leader starts out well-intentioned but succumbs to the pressure of forces that seek to co-opt the leader's power and influence for their own selfish gain.

We have all seen various examples of how insincerity shapes poor leadership actions and outcomes. For example, some people seek public office to enrich themselves through corrupt practices or influence peddling; some political leaders enact policies solely geared towards winning them re-election as opposed to providing long-term benefits to their constituents; some heads of corporations enact corporate policies that benefit the company's short term stock performance and their own executive bonus potential, to the detriment of employees and other stakeholders. In Islamic organizations and socio-religious groups, some people seek office motivated by the desire for fame and prestige. In these and many other cases, the leader's purpose becomes primarily one of trying to benefit himself, and his subsequent actions are shaped largely by that motivation. This insincerity often leads to suboptimal performance in-terms of fulfilling the goals of the group and bringing benefit to it.

Thus, we find numerous commandments in the Qur'an emphasizing the necessity of having a sincere purpose:

قُلْ إِنِّي أُمِرْتُ أَنْ أَعْبُدَ اللَّهَ مُخْلِصًا لَّهُ الدِّينَ

Say: "Verily, I am commanded to serve Allah with sincere devotion; -Az-zumar 39:11

قُلِ اللَّهَ أَعْبُدُ مُخْلِصًا لَّهُ دِينِي (39:14)

Say: "It is Allah I serve, with my sincere (and exclusive) devotion" - Az-zumar 39:14

وَمَا أُمِرُوا إِلَّا لِيَعْبُدُوا اللَّهَ مُخْلِصِينَ لَهُ الدِّينَ حُنَفَاء وَيُقِيمُوا الصَّلَاةَ وَيُؤْتُوا الزَّكَاةَ وَذَلِكَ دِينُ الْقَيِّمَةِ (98:5)

And they have been commanded no more than this: To worship Allah, offering Him sincere devotion, being true (in faith); to establish regular prayer; and to practice regular charity; and that is the Religion Right and Straight. – Al-Bayyinah 98:5

Prophet Muhammad (saw), said: *"No servant is given authority by Allah and he does not fulfill its duties sincerely but that he will never smell the fragrance of Paradise."* In another narration, the Prophet (saw) said, *"Allah will forbid him from entering Paradise."* - Sahih Al-Bukhari/Sahih Muslim

Thus, for a Muslim, the seemingly mundane act of leadership over any type of entity (political, religious, business, social, et cetera), is considered a religious duty for which God rewards him for sincere service and holds him to account for doing otherwise. In this respect, a leader cannot hope to be good and sincere only within a religious context, while acting avariciously in other situations. That sort of duplicity is disavowed by God and condemned in all ethical value-systems (secular and religious). Prophet Muhammad (saw), would deny leadership appointments to those he either deemed incapable of fulfilling its duties (as in the previously cited case of Abu Dharr, an honorable companion), and more frequently, in the case of those he deemed insincere in their desires for office.

Do we then advocate that a leader's service should be wholly altruistic, and that they should not gain any benefit from their service? Far from it. Everyone is entitled to fair compensation for their service, and leaders should be rewarded commensurate with the value they provide to the organization. There is nothing wrong in aspiring to leadership positions, or desiring growth and advancement, as long as one approaches it with the intention of fully performing its duties and puts the interest of the group above any selfish interest. Those charged with appointing officials into positions of leadership are also expected to be discerning and careful in the choice of candidates they put forth, and to ensure that those chosen are encouraged to approach their duties with the utmost sincerity and integrity (more on the topic of integrity later).

Caliph Ali, in advising Malik Al-Ashtar on the appointment of Chief Justices, said:

"Once you have selected the right man for the office, pay him handsomely enough, to let him live in comfort and in keeping with his position, enough to keep him above temptations. Give him a position in your court so high none can even dream of coveting it and so high that neither back-biting nor intrigue can touch him".

Thus, being legitimately rewarded for their service does not contradict the requirement for leaders to be sincere in fulling the duties of the position and being true in their commitments to the group.

Benefits

Sincerity fosters a sense of accountability in the leader and helps develop humility in him. The sincere leader is better able to lead without fear or favor and to uphold justice. They are stronger in their commitment to the attainment of the group's objectives and more apt to do what is required towards that end. Followers are also more likely to support a leader whose motivations are perceived to be higher than his own self-interest. People are quick to recognize a sincere leader from one who is only in it for his own gain. When people know or suspect that the person at the top is only in it for himself, they are more likely to act selfishly as well as it then becomes a case of "everyman for himself". This leads to corruption and disaffection in the rank and file of the organization.

Finally, we should remember that Allah rewards sincere service, even when the outcome falls short of the goal. People are also more understanding and accepting of a leader's failings if the leader is deemed sincere in his efforts and commitment to the served.

Chapter 4: Being Servant Leaders

F undamental to the concept of leadership in Islam is the idea of leadership as a service. This concept is reflected in the saying of Prophet Muhammad (saw) that:

"A leader of a people is their servant" – Abu Dawud

Leadership as taught in Islam, and as practiced by Prophet Muhammad (saw), and by many of the great leaders after him, exemplifies the idea of servant leadership, wherein a leader's purpose and fundamental responsibility is to fulfil the legitimate needs of the community that he serves and to guide them in the attainment of their beneficial objectives. A leader's purpose is to serve his stakeholders, not to be served by them. Rather he serves and is devoted to them.

This concept is closely aligned with the principle and habit of sincerity of purpose we discussed earlier, since a leader is only able to approach leadership as a service when their purpose for assuming the leadership role is genuinely to fulfill its requirements and to benefit those they lead (without prejudice to the expectation of a just recompense for the leader's efforts).

Since the publication of Robert K. Greenleaf's classic, "*Servant Leadership*" in the seventies, there has been a powerful movement to promote the concept of servant leadership in the business world and beyond. This concept, itself inspired by a character in Herman Hesse's novel, "*A Journey to the East*", focuses on the altruistic nature of leadership, and the leader as a servant by nature. Both works have their linkage to the Islamic concept of servant leadership, though not directly acknowledged in either works.

The principle of servant leadership requires a fundamental mental shift in how we view the relationship of the leader to the group (i.e. the dynamics of power, responsibility and accountability in the group, as well as ownership and control of group resources). In traditional leadership structures, the leader views his position as one wherein he is entitled to be served *by* the group; his actions as a leader spring from this fundamental notion and hence, the group's interest becomes subordinate to his own. This is of course manifested differently in different group structures. For example, in a political dictatorship or autocracy, the worst of this kind of leadership form can be easily observed in the autocratic, corrupt and unjust actions of the leader, whereas in matured democracies, the ills of this approach to leadership are often well masked and less obvious to all (but nonetheless present).

Islamic values require that leadership be viewed and practiced as a service by the one in the position of leadership for the benefit of the group. The leader's actions then spring from this precept and is shaped by the desire to be true in servitude to the group. When one thinks of leadership as a service to the led, one is more likely to make decisions and take actions with the interest of the constituents at the forefront of one's consideration, and more likely to exert oneself to potential. A servant leader is also by nature humble in the exercise of the power and privilege his position confers on him, and would view himself as a mere custodian, rather than owner, of the group's resources. A servant leader leads from the front by being the first to demonstrate the qualities and actions they expect of their constituents and inspires them by action (rather than by just words). The servant leader protects the led, creating an environment for them to grow and thrive, and shielding them from both internal and external threats.

The Prophet (saw) said: *"Verily, the leader is only a shield behind whom they fight, and he protects them. If he commands the fear of Allah the Exalted and justice, then he will have a reward. If he commands something else, then it will be against him."* - Sahih Muslim

In a corporation, an effective servant leader acts as the shield behind which his team operates by providing them the support and political cover to navigate organizational politics and bureaucracy to get their work done. A parent shields the family from the socio-economic vicissitudes of life as best as they can, and an Imam or spiritual leader ministers to the spiritual needs of the community and strives to help them cope and respond to the various forces, spiritual, emotional, and others, that buffet their lives and threaten to undermine their faith and well-being.

Prophet Muhammad (saw) and the early successors (caliphs) after him demonstrated the practice of servant leadership to the highest degree and in practicing the ideals of servant leadership, there are no better role models. Muhammad (saw), led the community in action, and exerted himself in the service of the people, spiritually and physically, whether it's in walking the streets of the capital city of Madinah to get a pulse on the state of affairs of the people, joining in the digging of a trench to protect the city during an enemy siege, or being in the thick of action during a military campaign. He was likewise a family man, and a leader at home, busying himself in the service of his family and helping them with household chores after a grueling day of running the affairs of the state and catering to the needs of the people.

Similarly, Caliph Umar made it a key element of his administration to personally stay connected with the affairs of the people, wandering the streets of Madinah and the market place, and visiting the territories under the control of the government to take account of the state of affairs of his people, and to provide immediate remedies to their concerns where possible.

Benefits

Approaching the task of leadership as a service to the led fundamentally changes how the leadership role plays out. A servant leader will use the people's interests as the guiding principles for his actions and would exert himself towards attaining those interests. This greatly increases his chances of success in his role and earns him divine favor. People are also more apt to follow, make sacrifices, and show loyalty and support for a leader when he leads from the front by doing what he states, mirroring the qualities that he espouses, and by being, through his actions and conduct, the change he advocates for.

Chapter 5: Leading with Integrity

Integrity, defined as the quality of being honest and having and exhibiting moral uprightness, is an important quality that we all cherish in the people that we deal with, particularly our leaders. It is the quality that, when present in a leader, assures us that they will act with the outmost sincerity and honesty. We recognize that it is personal integrity that keeps a person from succumbing to any number of forces that would seek to sway them from adhering to the values and principles they profess, and to resist the temptation to act in ways inimical to the interest of the group for their own selfish benefit.

The principle of integrity is closely linked with many of the other habits of effective and ethical leadership we talk about in this book. To act with integrity entails starting out with and maintaining sincerity of purpose and recognizing that one's service is for the benefit of the people (i.e. being a servant leader). Also, a leader's words and actions should be in alignment, and he should be transparent in his actions to enable people correctly understand his motivations and correctly interpret his actions. Not only must the leader be honest in respect of themselves, they also need to act fairly and with integrity with respect to other people, ensuring that their actions do not unfairly harm or benefit anyone (i.e. act justly). Nepotism must be eschewed, as should any form of behavior that unfairly favors one group over another.

A leader should strive to be both above reproach in their actions and to be seen as such. Hence, it is not sufficient just to be honest; one's actions should also be clear and free of the kind of ambiguity that could prompt people to suspect the leader of ill motives or illicit actions. Opacity in motive and action breed suspicion that is often capitalized upon by those who oppose the leader and would seek to sow dissension within the group, or otherwise undermine the authority and influence of the leader.

Islam puts a great deal of emphasis on truthfulness and integrity, linking it directly to faith. The reward of being truthful, in faith and action, is described in the Qur'an thus:

قَالَ اللّٰهُ هَذَا يَوْمُ يَنفَعُ الصَّادِقِينَ صِدْقُهُمْ لَهُمْ

جَنَّاتٌ تَجْرِي مِن تَحْتِهَا الأَنْهَارُ خَالِدِينَ فِيهَا أَبَدًا

رَّضِيَ اللّٰهُ عَنْهُمْ وَرَضُوا عَنْهُ ذَلِكَ الْفَوْزُ الْعَظِيمُ

Allah will say: "This is a day on which the truthful will profit from their truth: theirs are gardens, with rivers flowing beneath, - their eternal Home: Allah well-pleased with them, and they with Allah. That is the great salvation, (the fulfilment of all desires). - Al-Ma'idah 5:119

لِيَجْزِيَ اللَّهُ الصَّادِقِينَ بِصِدْقِهِمْ وَيُعَذِّبَ الْمُنَافِقِينَ إِن شَاء أَوْ يَتُوبَ عَلَيْهِمْ إِنَّ اللَّهَ كَانَ غَفُورًا رَّحِيمًا

That Allah may reward the men of Truth for their Truth, and punish the Hypocrites if that be His Will, or turn to them in Mercy: for Allah is Oft-Forgiving, Most Merciful. - Al-Ahzab 33:24

Allah also denounces those who lack integrity and act fraudulently giving to people less than their due measures, while ironically demanding full recompense for themselves from others:

وَيْلٌ لِّلْمُطَفِّفِينَ الَّذِينَ إِذَا اكْتَالُواْ عَلَى النَّاسِ يَسْتَوْفُونَ

34

وَإِذَا كَالُوهُمْ أَو وَّزَنُوهُمْ يُخْسِرُونَ

أَلَا يَظُنُّ أُولَئِكَ أَنَّهُم مَّبْعُوثُونَ

لِيَوْمٍ عَظِيمٍ يَوْمَ يَقُومُ النَّاسُ لِرَبِّ الْعَالَمِينَ

Woe to those that deal in fraud, - Those who, when they have to receive by measure from men, exact full measure, but when they have to give by measure or weight to men, give less than due. Do they not think that they will be called to account? -On a Mighty Day, A Day when (all) mankind will stand before the Lord of the Worlds? - Al-Mutaffifin 83:1-6

The Prophet (saw) and the successors and other generation of Muslim leaders, took this directive for integrity so much to heart that many of the leaders would not use facilities paid for by public funds for their own personal needs (for example, not using a lamp fueled using public funds for personal errands or religious practices such as reading the Qur'an).

Dishonesty and lack of integrity were very much disliked by the Prophet (saw), that Aisha reported: "*There was no behavior more hateful to the Messenger of Allah, peace and blessings be upon him, than dishonesty. A man would tell a lie when speaking in the presence of the Prophet and he would not be satisfied until he knew that he had repented.*" - Sunan At-Tirmidhi

Unfortunately, people have grown to be skeptical of leaders and treat their words and actions with mistrust. This is reflective of the negative experience of dishonest leadership that people have experienced in different aspects of life throughout history. The Prophet (saw), strongly admonished against dishonesty, saying:

"You must be truthful. Verily, truthfulness leads to righteousness and righteousness leads to Paradise. A man continues to be truthful and encourages honesty until he is recorded with Allah as truthful. And beware of falsehood. Verily, falsehood leads to wickedness and wickedness leads to the Hellfire. A man continues to tell lies and encourages falsehood until he is recorded with Allah as a liar." - Sahih Al-Bukhari/Sahih Muslim

"Every traitor will have a flag on the Day of Judgement to identify them according to the amount of their treachery; there is no traitor of greater treachery than the leader of the people." – Sahih Al-Bukhari/Sahih Muslim

Benefits

Integrity is a core requirement of effective leadership (and of decent human co-existence). When leaders act with integrity, they make decisions and choices that are aligned with the interest of those they serve, even when doing so is difficult, and at the risk of missed unfair benefits to themselves. They also earn the trust, strong support and respect of their followers.

Chapter 6: Communicating with Impact

The ability to communicate effectively is one of the more obvious effective leadership competencies, but unfortunately it is also one that many leaders struggle with.

Communicating effectively means conveying information or ideas to others with the clarity and conciseness that enables them to have an easy and complete understanding of the intended message. Communication is effective when the message is understood by its audience as it is desired to be, and when the message has the intended impact or effect on the audience.

There are a few crucial elements of effective communication, and it is important that each of these be taken into account in order to communicate effectively. We will explore the importance of intentionality in communication and also how the words used, the tone of the message, body language or posture (in the case of verbal communication), as well as the context in which the communication occurs, all influence the audience's receptivity to the message.

Several verses of the Qur'an offer teachings on how to communicate effectively and we see these communication principles put to use in the life of the Prophet (saw), the successors and other great leaders. Prophet Muhammad (saw) was a master communicator and demonstrated many of the key principles of communication that we will discuss in this chapter.

Clear Purpose or Intentionality

A leader should be deliberate and intentional in their communication and clear as to their purpose. In other words, one should start out with an understanding of the purpose behind the message one wants to convey, and the effect one wants to achieve with it. Having a clear understanding of that purpose helps in framing the message in the most effective way. One should avoid frivolity in communication and recognize the capacity for our words to spur actions towards goodness, or to incite towards harm and evil. Islam teaches that the purpose behind our communication should be beneficial and not sinful. The following ahadith provide reminders in that respect:

"The greatest propensity for good or evil in a man lies between his two lips," meaning his tongue. – Sahih Ibn Hibban

"Whomsoever believe in Allah and His messenger should speak good or keep quiet" – Sahih Muslim

Truthfulness and honesty in communication is also an important quality of ethical leaders. Leaders should safeguard their integrity by being truthful and avoiding deceptiveness in their communication even when being honest might seem difficult:

يَا أَيُّهَا الَّذِينَ آمَنُوا اتَّقُوا اللَّهَ وَقُولُوا قَوْلًا سَدِيدًا

O you who have attained to faith! Remain conscious of God, and [always] speak with a will to bring out [only] what is just and true – Al-Ahzab 33:70

Abu Sa'id al-Khudri reported: The Prophet, peace and blessings be upon him, said, *"Let not fear of the people prevent one of you from speaking the truth, if he knows it."* - Musnad Ahmad

Choice of Words

This is what most people focus on almost exclusively when thinking about improving their communication skills. While our choice of words matters greatly, it still only accounts for a small percentage of communication effectiveness, according to studies on the subject. Nonetheless, it is important to use words that aid the easy delivery of the intended message. The choice of words one uses should match the audience, both in terms of the language used as well as the vocabulary and level of linguistic sophistication employed. Speaking or writing to a general audience requires the use of language that can be easily comprehended by the average member of that group, whereas the same message directed at a group of academics or business executives will take on a decidedly more formal and perhaps, sophisticated form. Using the vocabulary common amongst the audience will aid their comprehension and help the speaker or writer in building rapport with the audience. The message being delivered should be communicated in a manner that matches the audience's knowledge and experience. The importance of this is illustrated in the advice of Caliph Ali:

"Speak to people only according to their level of knowledge. Would you like for Allah and His Messenger to be denied (because of their being unable to understand)?" - Sahih al-Bukhari

The choice of words should also match the intended impact and seek to evoke in the audience the effects or emotions that the communicator desires. Whether in a casual conversation or in proselytizing, it is important to use kind and gentle words to address the audience, as demonstrated in the following verse of the Qur'an:

ادْعُ إِلَى سَبِيلِ رَبِّكَ بِالْحِكْمَةِ وَالْمَوْعِظَةِ الْحَسَنَةِ وَجَادِلْهُم بِالَّتِي هِيَ أَحْسَنُ إِنَّ رَبَّكَ هُوَ أَعْلَمُ بِمَن ضَلَّ عَن سَبِيلِهِ وَهُوَ أَعْلَمُ بِالْمُهْتَدِينَ

Invite (all) to the Way of thy Lord with wisdom and beautiful exhortation; and argue with them in ways that are best and most gracious: for thy Lord knoweth best, who have strayed from His Path, and who receive guidance. – An-Nahl 16:125

Similar advice can be seen in Allah's commandment to Prophets Musa (Moses) and Haroun (Haroun, his brother) on how they should approach and address the fearsome Fir'aun (Pharoah):

فَقُولَا لَهُ قَوْلًا لَّيِّنًا لَّعَلَّهُ يَتَذَكَّرُ أَوْ يَخْشَى

"and speak to him gently, perhaps he may take heed or fear (Allah)." Taha 20:44

Allah warns in the Quran against using insulting, obscene or sarcastic language in speech:

يَا أَيُّهَا الَّذِينَ آمَنُوا لَا يَسْخَرْ قَوْمٌ مِّن قَوْمٍ عَسَى

أَن يَكُونُوا خَيْرًا مِّنْهُمْ وَلَا نِسَاء مِّن نِّسَاء عَسَى أَن

يَكُنَّ خَيْرًا مِّنْهُنَّ وَلَا تَلْمِزُوا أَنفُسَكُمْ وَلَا تَنَابَزُوا

بِالْأَلْقَابِ بِئْسَ الاِسْمُ الْفُسُوقُ بَعْدَ الْإِيمَانِ وَمَن لَّمْ

يَتُبْ فَأُوْلَئِكَ هُمُ الظَّالِمُونَ

O YOU who have attained to faith! No men shall deride [other] men: it may well be that those [whom they deride] are better than themselves; and no women [shall deride other] women: it may well be that those [whom they deride] are better than themselves. And neither shall you defame one another, nor insult one another by [opprobrious] epithets: evil is all imputation of iniquity after [one has attained to] faith; and they who [become guilty thereof and] do not repent - it is they, they who are evildoers! – Al-Hujurat 49:11

It is advisable to avoid words that malign and alienate others. Harsh, disparaging language tends to create resentment to the message and the messenger, and often fails to produce the beneficial impact that might have been intended, whereas, criticism or feedback that is worded in non-disparaging language is more likely to be heeded. An excellent advice from the great scholar, Imam Al-Shafi'I illustrates this point:

Al-Muzanni reported: Al-Shafi'i, may Allah have mercy on him, heard me one day as I said, "This narrator is a great liar!" Al-Shafi'i said to me, "O Abu Ibrahim, dress your words in the best manner. Do not say this narrator is a great liar, but rather say his narrations are of no importance." - Fath al-Mughith

One should also be clear in what one says and avoid ambiguous and obscure words and phrasing that can confuse the audience or lead to wrong interpretations of the message.

Aisha reported: *The discourse of the Messenger of Allah, peace and blessings be upon him, was clear such that he was understood by everyone who heard him.* - Sunan Abi Dawud

Tonality

The tone in which a message is delivered could override the literal meaning of the words expressed. An audience uses the communicator's tone to infer the intention behind the message. For example, the tone of a message could make it come across as friendly, critical, demeaning, sarcastic, jocular, or insulting, whether or not that was the communicator's intended effect and irrespective of the literal meaning of the words used.

In speech, the tone is reflected in the vocal inflections (how the words are pronounced and emphasized) and the vocal volume. This is influenced by the speaker's emotions (anger, fear, affection, etc.) during the communication episode, their perception of the relationship with the audience (friends, adversaries, superiors, subordinates, etc.) and the effect they intend to have with the message. Effective communication thus requires being mindful of one's tone when speaking and writing, and striving to match how we express our message with the understanding and impact we want our audience to get from the message. A few key suggestions to note in this respect:

Match your tone to the audience and event: for example, how you address a group of teammates might be different from how you should address your company's board of directors since dealing with the latter group likely requires a bit more formality.

Be aware of cultural nuances in tonality: some cultures are very big in outward show of respect, even in business settings, and this applies to how people address each other (compare the highly reverential Japanese business culture to the more informal American attitudes).

How you feel on the inside can show up in your tone, despite your best efforts: when emotionally distressed or upset, consider delaying speaking or writing, in order for your words and tone not to betray your negative and potentially destructive emotions.

Maintaining a vocal volume appropriate to the setting is also important. This means generally being moderate in volume and matching the sound level to the environment. Heed the advice in the following verse of the Qur'an:

$$\text{وَاقْصِدْ فِي مَشْيِكَ وَاغْضُضْ مِن صَوْتِكَ إِنَّ أَنكَرَ الْأَصْوَاتِ لَصَوْتُ الْحَمِيرِ}$$

"Hence, be modest in thy bearing, and lower thy voice: for, behold, the ugliest of all voices is the [loud] voice of asses..." - Luqman 31:19

Body Language

Our verbal communication is affected by signals we send knowingly or otherwise via our body language. The audience consciously or subconsciously checks for agreement between the words we utter and the signals we give off. If there is a mismatch in the signals and the words being uttered, the audience is likely to doubt the credibility of the speaker or to be less inclined to act on the intended request or instruction. Body language includes facial expressions (including the less obvious micro-expressions that are harder to control or feign), eye contact and movement, body posture (how we sit, stand, or position our limbs), and hand gestures. Effective communicators use their body language to aid the delivery of their message.

Neuroscience research suggests that matching the audience's body language (particularly in one-on-one interactions) activates mirror neurons in the audience's brains and helps to establish rapport with them. This matching includes assuming similar body posture and facial expressions, without obvious mimicry (which could be downright odd or off-putting to the audience). Smiling is also essential in building rapport with one's audience. A sincere smile goes a long way in making the audience feel comfortable and receptive to the message. This was a common practice of the Prophet (saw):

"Abdullah ibn al-Harith reported: *I have not seen anyone smile more often than the Messenger of Allah, peace and blessings be upon him.*" - Sunan At-Tirmidhi

Effective communicators try to "read" their audience (i.e. take note of the audience's facial expressions, body language, tone, etc.) and adjust their message and delivery style appropriately.

Appropriate touching can also aid in communication effectiveness. For example, placing the hand on someone's shoulder or arm can signal friendship and trust in some contexts. However, great care is called for to ensure that the relationship with the audience is such that would allow for such physical contact (particularly across gender, where it is almost always inadvisable to do so).

Context – Place, Time and Situation

Choosing the right context to deliver a message can greatly influence the audience's receptivity to it. Hence, one of the key considerations a leader must have is matching the message to the appropriate context in terms of time, place, and situation. For example, delivering important feedback to an angry person might be much less effective than waiting for their anger to subside; providing feedback to someone in private is generally better than doing so in public; saving a critical or serious message for a time when the audience is in somber mood might be more beneficial than addressing them when they are engaged in playful endeavors.

Other Considerations

Think before speaking: Emotional intelligence is an important quality of effective leaders, and this quality (or lack thereof) is apparent in how measured and deliberate a leader is in their speech. Al-Bayhaqi reported:

Hassan Al-Basri, may Allah have mercy on him, said, *"The intelligent man has his tongue behind his heart. If he intends to say something, he consults his heart whether he should say it or be silent. The foolish man has his tongue in front of his heart. If he intends to say something, he lets his tongue speak first."* - Shu'ab Al-Iman

Knowing when to speak is as important as knowing what to say and how to say it. Being thoughtful in one's communication helps to ensure maximum effectiveness, prevent gaffs, and project confidence and wisdom.

Listen Actively: A crucial aspect of communication is listening to the other party. Just as a speaker wants to be heard and understood by the audience, they must also strive to hear and understand the other party. Listening actively includes avoiding distractions, showing presence with the body language (making eye contact with the audience and turning the whole body towards them, etc.), and asking questions or repeating back parts of the conversation for clarity (when appropriate).

Brevity trumps verbosity: In general, it is best to keep a message short and devoid of frivolities, as people's attention spans tend to be very short and they are likely to tune out the message if it is unduly long. The Prophet (saw) would keep his speeches very short and urged the believers to do the same. Most of his khutbahs (sermons) were short (with the notable exception of his farewell sermon). The caliphs after him also recognized the importance of brevity in communication as evident in Caliph Abu Bakr's inaugural address quoted earlier. We also see in the following ahadith this same principle demonstrated:

'Ammar reported: The Messenger of Allah, peace and blessings be upon him, said, *"Verily, the length of a man's prayer and the brevity of his sermon is a sign of his understanding. Lengthen the prayer and shorten the sermon. Verily, some eloquence is charming."* -Sahih Muslim

Ibn Umar reported: *I said, "O Messenger of Allah, give me a word and make it short that I might understand it." The Messenger of Allah, peace and blessings be upon him, said, "Do not be angry." I repeated my question twice and each time the Prophet responded, "Do not be angry."* - Musnad Abi Ya'la

Use stories, imagery, and visual cues: Stories and imagery can be very effective communication tools as they help the audience to better grasp abstract concepts and to remember the message better. Physical props (message-relevant objects) and visual aids are also excellent learning and communication tools, particularly with an audience of visual learners (which most people are to varying degrees).

The prophet (saw) would occasionally draw diagrams in the sand to illustrate concepts he was explaining to his audience, as he would also use analogies, parables and stories to explain his message. In many verses of the Qur'an, Allah Most High uses imagery, analogies, and stories to illustrate Islamic teachings, as illustrated in the verse below:

وَلَوْ شِئْنَا لَرَفَعْنَاهُ بِهَا وَلَكِنَّهُ أَخْلَدَ إِلَى الْأَرْضِ وَاتَّبَعَ هَوَاهُ فَمَثَلُهُ كَمَثَلِ الْكَلْبِ إِن تَحْمِلْ عَلَيْهِ يَلْهَثْ أَوْ تَتْرُكْهُ يَلْهَث ذَّلِكَ مَثَلُ الْقَوْمِ الَّذِينَ كَذَّبُواْ بِآيَاتِنَا فَاقْصُصِ الْقَصَصَ لَعَلَّهُمْ يَتَفَكَّرُونَ

If it had been Our will, We should have elevated him with Our signs; but he inclined to the earth, and followed his own vain desires. His similitude is that of a dog: if you attack him, he lolls out his tongue, or if you leave him alone, he (still) lolls out his tongue. That is the similitude of those who reject Our signs; So relate the story; perchance they may reflect. - Al-A'raf 7:176

Thus, a leader should learn to be a good storyteller as stories can be immensely powerful in communicating a message and fostering retention.

Reinforce with repetition: Anas ibn Malik reported: *When the Prophet, peace and blessings be upon him, would speak, he would repeat himself three times until he was understood. Whenever he came to people and greeted them with peace, he would greet them three times.* - Sahih Al-Bukhari

Value silence and reticence over frivolities: Abu Umamah reported: The Prophet, peace and blessings be upon him, said, *"Modesty and reticence are two branches of faith. Profanity and temerity are two branches of hypocrisy."* - Sunan At-Tirmidhi

Imam At-Tirmidhi said, *"Reticence is to speak little. Profanity is to speak obscenely. Temerity is to speak too often, such as those preachers who preach at great length and with eloquence, to be praised by people in what is not pleasing to Allah."*

Benefits

The ability to communicate effectively is an important leadership quality. How a message is delivered greatly influences the audience's receptivity to it and leaders must learn how to communicate properly, whether in one-on-one settings or to a large audience, and whether in writing or in speeches and conversations. The valuable work a leader does can be greatly undermined by an inability to communicate effectively. Hence, using the principles explained above will assist leaders to get the message across and to influence their audience.

Chapter 7: Dealing Justly with All

Justice is a cornerstone principle of civilized and secure coexistence in any society or organization. It is the principle by which members are assured that their interests are protected, that they will get their just dues, and that members of the group do not deal unfairly with each other without consequences. Justice entails acting with equity towards all, in all matters, big and small. It also means avoiding discrimination on various bases, including race, ethnicity, social class and religion.

Justices is one of the attributes of Allah and a quality that Allah demands of his creations in their dealings with each other. Allah says in the Qur'an:

إِنَّ اللّهَ يَأْمُرُ بِالْعَدْلِ وَالإِحْسَانِ وَإِيتَاء ذِي الْقُرْبَى وَيَنْهَى عَنِ الْفَحْشَاء وَالْمُنكَرِ وَالْبَغْيِ يَعِظُكُمْ لَعَلَّكُمْ تَذَكَّرُونَ

BEHOLD, God enjoins justice, and the doing of good, and generosity towards [one's] fellow-men; and He forbids all that is shameful and all that runs counter to reason, as well as envy; [and] He exhorts [repeatedly] so that you might bear [all this] in mind. – An-Nahl 16:90

Just and fair dealing is expected of everyone, and particularly, of the leader, as he has an outsized influence over the life and well-being of those he serves, and is in a position of power and authority to make decisions on the allocation of resources, positions, benefits, as well as the administration of justice between them. He is expected to deal justly even when his own interests, or that of those close to him are at stake. The leader's actions must similarly be without fear or favor towards certain members of the group, nor be influenced by dislike or hatred of others:

يَا أَيُّهَا الَّذِينَ آمَنُواْ كُونُواْ قَوَّامِينَ بِالْقِسْطِ شُهَدَاء لِلّهِ وَلَوْ عَلَى أَنفُسِكُمْ أَوِ الْوَالِدَيْنِ وَالأَقْرَبِينَ إِن يَكُنْ غَنِيًّا أَوْ فَقَيرًا فَاللّهُ أَوْلَى بِهِمَا فَلاَتَتَّبِعُواْ الْهَوَى أَن تَعْدِلُواْ وَإِن تَلْوُواْ أَوْ تُعْرِضُواْ فَإِنَّ اللّهَ كَانَ بِمَا تَعْمَلُونَ خَبِيرًا

55

O YOU who have attained to faith! Be ever steadfast in upholding equity, bearing witness to the truth for the sake of God, even though it be against your own selves or your parents and kinsfolk. Whether the person concerned be rich or poor, God's claim takes precedence over [the claims of] either of them. Do not, then, follow your own desires, lest you swerve from justice: for if you distort [the truth], behold, God is indeed aware of all that you do! – An-Nisa 4:135

Just dealing is considered a sign of outmost God-consciousness, one without which any proclamation to being righteous is mere words:

يَا أَيُّهَا الَّذِينَ آمَنُواْ كُونُواْ قَوَّامِينَ لِلّهِ شُهَدَاء بِالْقِسْطِ وَلاَ يَجْرِمَنَّكُمْ شَنَآنُ قَوْمٍ عَلَى أَلاَّ تَعْدِلُواْ اعْدِلُواْ هُوَ أَقْرَبُ لِلتَّقْوَى وَاتَّقُواْ اللّهَ إِنَّ اللّهَ خَبِيرٌ بِمَا تَعْمَلُونَ

O YOU who have attained to faith! Be ever steadfast in your devotion to God, bearing witness to the truth in all equity; and never let hatred of any-one lead you into the sin of deviating from justice. Be just: this is closest to being God-conscious. And remain conscious of God: verily, God is aware of all that you do. – Al-Ma'idah 5:8

إِنَّ اللهَ يَأْمُرُكُمْ أَن تُؤَدُّواْ الأَمَانَاتِ إِلَى أَهْلِهَا وَإِذَا حَكَمْتُم بَيْنَ النَّاسِ أَن تَحْكُمُواْ بِالْعَدْلِ إِنَّ اللّهَ نِعِمَّا يَعِظُكُم بِهِ إِنَّ اللّهَ كَانَ سَمِيعًا بَصِيرًا

BEHOLD, God bids you to deliver all that you have been entrusted with unto those who are entitled thereto, and whenever you judge between people, to judge with justice. Verily, most excellent is what God exhorts you to do: verily, God is all-hearing, all-seeing! – An-Nisa 4:58

Prophet Muhammad (saw), explained the virtue of upholding justice by mentioning that God will elevate an unbelieving nation in rank over one which professes faith but does not uphold justice. He extoled the virtue of upholding justice above mere rituals of worship:

"A day of just leadership is better than sixty years of worship, and a legal limit properly established in the land is purer for it than forty days of rain." - Al-Sunan Al-Kubra

He similarly cautioned leaders against acting unjustly, saying:

"No one who is placed in leadership over 10 or more, then does not act justly between them, except that on the Day of Judgement he is brought in shackles and chains" – Hakim

A leader must be mindful of how their actions and policies impact the different members of their constituencies to ensure that some members are not unduly favored or harmed by such, and that everyone has access to seek redress for any perceived wrong done to them. The leader also must ensure that opportunities are made equally available, while being mindful to correct foundational inequities that might perpetuate injustice and unequal access to opportunities within the group.

Benefits

A society or organization that is based on just dealings amongst its members will enjoy social harmony, stability and solidarity amongst its members, and strong loyalty to the leaders and the institution.

Chapter 8: Developing and Maintaining Trust

Trust is the fabric that ties human relations together. Human relations and transactions are largely built on some measure of implicit and explicit trust. For us to live together in society, there must be implied trust in our ability to live together to our mutual benefit. There is implied trust in our safety in society and in the structures that are setup to provide for our security and well-being. When we transact with each other for goods and services, there is enough implied trust that such transaction would be to our mutual benefit and that we would not be harmed by it.

Effective leadership requires that the leader build and maintain the trust of the people he or she leads, for to willingly follow someone requires trusting in their ability, capacity, and willingness to do the job and to do right by one. People will not willingly follow or support a leader if they do not trust in his ability to lead and desire to bring benefit to them.

Trust however is a quality that must be earned through sustained set of practices and behaviors on the part of the leader but can be quickly eroded if the leader fails to consciously strive to develop and nurture a relationship of trust with his community. For trust to develop and be sustained, the leader needs to:

- Treat trust-building as a continuous exercise
- Act with truthfulness and integrity (qualities we discussed earlier)
- Be transparent in his actions (people see actions and results, not intentions)
- Be selfless and just in his dealings with people

Islam emphasizes trust as one of the important qualities of a good character, and a sign of faith. Prophet Muhammad (saw) said:

"The believer is one who is trusted by people." - Sahih Ibn Hibban

"There is no faith for one who cannot be trusted. There is no religion for one who cannot keep a promise."- Musnad Ahmad

Being trustworthy is a character of a believer and of an effective leader, and a measure of a "man". Caliph Umar ibn al-Khattab said:

"Do not let yourselves be impressed by the roar of a man. Rather, if he fulfills the trust and restrains himself from harming the honor of people, he will truly be a man." - Al-Zuhd wal-Raqa'iq

A leader must strive to build and sustain trust with the people. Trust is hard won but easy to erode. A leader must act in ways that enables people to trust him. This includes being truthful with his words, faithful to his promises, transparent in his actions, and acting with sincerity, integrity, and dealing fairly with all.

Benefits

Leading people effectively requires that they accept and trust in the ability of the leader to lead them and to serve their interests. Leaders that earn the trust of their followers enjoy their steadfast support and loyalty, and benefit from a bigger demonstration of discretionary effort and willingness to endure and sacrifice for the long-term benefit of the group. Also, actively striving to cultivate the people's trust helps the leader to focus on effective leadership practices and the interests of the people he serves.

Chapter 9: Engaging in Participative Leadership

L eaders are human, with human frailties and limited capabilities, knowledge and experience. A big part of leadership involves making decisions for the group, influencing what policies get enacted, how the group's limited resources are allocated, and how to combat threats to the group's interests. A leader's decisions and actions have an outsized influence and impact on the lives and well-being of the people he serves. Thus, the quality of those decisions plays a big role in the outcomes the leader achieves. Hence, availing oneself of the capabilities of other people helps to compensate for our own limitations and inexperience in certain aspects of life and leading.

A Participatory Leadership style is one wherein the leader involves others in deciding the affairs of the group, tapping into the collective wisdom, and incorporating the perspectives of others in deciding for the group. A leader involves the people he serves in deciding their affairs and well-being, and gives them both a say, and sense of ownership over matters that affect them. This is without prejudice to the leader's authority and overall responsibility to lead and command in service of the group. While a leader can have command and control authority over those he leads, he is not expected to be dictatorial in serving them. This participatory approach to leadership is a common practice of ethical and effective leaders.

An additional dimension of participatory leadership involves recognizing man's need for divine guidance in all his affairs. So, a participatory Muslim leader involves both God and other people in the performance of his leadership duties. Islam encourages everyone, leaders and followers, to seek help in their decision-making process by engaging in consultation. Consultation, via various mechanisms, is a key element of participatory leadership. Consultation is of two types – Seeking divine guidance (Istikhaarah) and seeking counsel of other people (Istishaarah). Both are considered important elements of a participatory leadership style in Islam.

Seeking Divine Guidance (Istikhaarah)

A Muslim acknowledges God's omniscience, and his own limited knowledge of the past and present, as well as his ignorance or uncertainty of what the future portends. Thus, praying for divine guidance in decision making is a key practice that Islam teaches, even with respect to mundane affairs of life (as what is seemingly mundane now could precipitate much larger effects in the future).

Praying for guidance does not negate the need for due diligence and critical thinking in decision making. It is also not meant to be a substitute for decisiveness in avoiding what is wrong or unethical. So, when the choice is between right and wrong moral choices, the decisive path forward for the leader is to do what is morally right. Praying for strength and courage to do so is of course highly recommended as taking the morally correct stance isn't always easy.

The Prophet (saw) used to teach the companions to perform Salatul istikhaarah (a special prayer for seeking divine guidance) in the same fashion as he would teach them the verses of the Qur'an. Similarly, expressing one's reliance on God through prayer is considered an act of worship. Also, recognizing the need to pray for guidance has a humbling and meditative effect on the leader, and puts him in a better frame of mind to process whatever decisions he has to make. It also helps to frame his choices, ensuring that the decisions he is about to make are ethical. It also gives the leader strong confidence in proceeding with execution, knowing that his decisions were made with much forethought and after prayers for guidance.

Consulting Others (Istishaarah)

Every leader should have access to both an inner circle of trusted and wise advisers, as well as have avenues for gauging popular sentiments. For example, a chief executive would need the assistance of competent heads of various divisions in his organization. At the same time, he needs to have a mechanism in place for gauging popular sentiments and attitudes in the organization he serves. Often, leaders hide themselves away in "ivory towers", surrounded by sycophants who deprive them of sincere counsel. Some leaders also demonstrate a lack of desire for counsel, or at least for counsel of the honest and sincere type, and those around quickly learn not to offer any.

An effective leader avails himself of the counsel of the honest and wise people around him. He actively seeks out those in positions to offer informed advice on various matters, whether official capacities (by appointing competent people into positions of authority and listening to them) or by engaging subject matter experts in a consulting role when required. The leader must also seek to reach beyond his leadership hierarchy in forming opinions about issues as those close officials are sometimes too far removed from the realities of the situations of the people to be objective or well informed.

Prophet Muhammad (saw) availed himself of the counsel of his companions on a variety of issues, whether through a voluntary offer of counsel by the companions, or the prophet (saw) himself initiating a consult as commanded in the Qur'an:

فَبِمَا رَحْمَةٍ مِّنَ اللهِ لِنتَ لَهُمْ وَلَوْ كُنتَ فَظًّا غَلِيظَ الْقَلْبِ لاَنفَضُّواْ مِنْ حَوْلِكَ فَاعْفُ عَنْهُمْ وَاسْتَغْفِرْ لَهُمْ وَشَاوِرْهُمْ فِي الأَمْرِ فَإِذَا عَزَمْتَ فَتَوَكَّلْ عَلَى اللهِ إِنَّ اللهَ يُحِبُّ الْمُتَوَكِّلِينَ (3:159)

It is part of the Mercy of Allah that thou dost deal gently with them Wert thou severe or harsh-hearted, they would have broken away from about thee: so pass over (their faults), and ask for (Allah's) forgiveness for them; and consult them in affairs (of moment). Then, when thou hast taken a decision put thy trust in Allah. For Allah loves those who put their trust (in Him). – Al-Imran 3:159

Allah also describes mutual consultation as a positive attribute of believers:

وَالَّذِينَ اسْتَجَابُوا لِرَبِّهِمْ وَأَقَامُوا الصَّلَاةَ وَأَمْرُهُمْ شُورَى بَيْنَهُمْ وَمِمَّا رَزَقْنَاهُمْ يُنفِقُونَ (42:38)

Those who hearken to their Lord, and establish regular Prayer; who (conduct) their affairs by mutual Consultation; who spend out of what We bestow on them for Sustenance; - 42:38

Islam also teaches that offering honest and sincere advice to the leader is a duty of the follower. It is not enough to criticize leaders for their shortcomings, while neglecting to offer them sincere advice on how they can do better. When a person is consulted, he is expected to give honest and sincere advice. The Messenger of Allah (saw) spoke variously on the importance of seeking and giving counsel.

"One is who is consulted is in a position of trust." - Sunan At-Tirmidhi

"If your brother requests your consultation, let him give counsel." - Sunan Ibn Majah

*"Allah is pleased with three things from you, and He is angry with three things from you. He is pleased that you worship Him and do not associate anything with Him, and that you take hold of the rope of Allah altogether (i.e. stay united), and **that you give good counsel to the one to whom Allah gives command over you**. He is angry with you for gossip, squandering property, and asking too many questions."* - Muwatta Malik

Caliph Umar Ibn Khattab (May Allah be pleased with him) advised:

"Seek the counsel of the righteous, for Allah Most High, says 'Of all His servants, only such as are endowed with [innate] knowledge stand [truly] in awe of God (Fatir 35:28)'"

A leader should seek divine guidance as well as the counsel of the wise, trustworthy ones around him and of those qualified to advise on the matter at hand, and then take decisive action, trusting in Allah.

Benefits

Seeking Allah's guidance in deciding between lawful options is an act of worship and a means of benefiting from divine wisdom. It also helps to strengthen the leader's resolve as he executes his decision knowing that he has sought Allah's guidance prior to acting. Consulting people also allows the leader to leverage the various perspectives and experiences of the people that he consults. He is also more likely to enjoy the support of his followers as they develop a sense of ownership of the decisions made by the body and show more commitment to achieving the intended outcome. They will also see the leader as someone that listens to and engages with others, rather than as an arrogant, self-serving know-it all or dictator.

Chapter 10: Possessing and Projecting a Positive Attitude

E ffective leadership can be hard to practice, and good leaders are often underappreciated and face seemingly insurmountable odds. Challenges a leader face can range from overcoming internal doubts about his or the groups capability to achieve the group's desired goals, to dealing with external and internal threats to his leadership and to the well-being of the group.

A political head has to work to implement his political agenda, deal with all manners of challenges associated with doing so, while wading off political threats to his leadership. A corporate leader has to woo customers, motivate the workforce, and convince shareholders that the company was headed in the right direction and capable of meeting its performance goals. A family head has to provide for the family, assure the family's present and future well-being, and shield members from the socio-economic challenges of the present and future. All of these and more make leading a very tasking venture. Leaders can become easily overwhelmed with the challenges of leadership and fall into despondency when their well-intentioned hard work does not yield the desired outcome, or when the people they serve act in ways that suggest a lack of appreciation for the leader's hard work and sacrifice.

To be effective despite these challenges, leaders must strive to remain optimistic about the prospects of achieving the goals of the group, and project optimism and determination for the group to see and be motivated by. They must learn to be positive and to keep their spirits up even when there does not seem to be much cause for optimism. They must:

- Have a positive expectation of Allah (i.e. believe that Allah is in control of the outcome and capable of turning around the direst of situations)
- Combine trust in Allah with intelligent, meaningful and decisive action
- Internalize optimism and put on a brave face even in the face of difficulty and when facing great odds

The leader should have firm faith in Allah and pray for Allah's assistance, with the positive expectation of God's benevolence, and steadfast belief in the truth of His promise of assistance to the faithful. He also needs to project confidence (while remaining humble) in the attainment, with the help of Allah, of the desired group objectives. The positive spirit and optimism of an effective leader is a powerful force that, as history has shown, can turn around negative attitudes in a group, and turn impending defeat into victory.

Many verses of the Qur'an explain the importance of trusting in Allah:

إِن يَنصُرْكُمُ اللّهُ فَلاَ غَالِبَ لَكُمْ وَإِن يَخْذُلْكُمْ فَمَن ذَا الَّذِي يَنصُرُكُم مِّن بَعْدِهِ وَعَلَى اللّهِ فَلْيَتَوَكِّلِ الْمُؤْمِنُونَ (3:160)

If Allah helps you, none can overcome you: If He forsakes you, who is there, after that, that can help you? in Allah, then, let believers put their trust. – Al-Imran 3:160

Also, we should remember that, while life is full of challenges, they can be overcome with persistence and perseverance:

فَإِنَّ مَعَ الْعُسْرِ يُسْرًا   إِنَّ مَعَ الْعُسْرِ ي

And, behold, with every hardship comes ease; verily, with every hardship comes ease! - Ash-Sharh 94:5-6

يَا أَيُّهَا الَّذِينَ آمَنُواْ اصْبِرُواْ وَصَابِرُواْ وَرَابِطُواْ وَاتَّقُواْ اللّهَ لَعَلَّكُمْ تُفْلِحُونَ

O you who have attained to faith! Be patient in adversity, and vie in patience with one another, and be ever ready [to do what is right], and remain conscious of God, so that you might attain to a happy state! - Al-Imran 3:200

While doing all they can to fulfil their governance responsibilities, a leader should put their trust in God and be consistent in the practice of seeking divine guidance and assistance and trusting in God's grace to come to their aid. An important requirement of the acceptance of supplication to God is hope and positive expectation of God's grace. Prophet Muhammad (saw) said: *"Call upon Allah with certainty that he will answer you. Know that Allah will not answer the supplication of a heart that is negligent and distracted."* - Sunan At-Tirmidhi

He (saw) also said: *"Verily, thinking well about Allah is a part of excellent worship of Allah."* - Sunan At-Tirmidhi

Finally, in a strong exhortation to remain positive and to have faith in God's grace, he (saw) said: *"Allah the Exalted says: I am as my servant expects me and I am with him as he remembers me"*. In another narration of this hadith, the Prophet (saw) said: *"Allah says: 'If he thinks good of me, he will have it. And if he thinks evil of me, he will have it'.*" - Sahih Al-Bukhari/Sahih Muslim

Optimism was a well-known quality of prophet Muhammad (saw), and of great leaders. He projected confidence in difficult situations, held out hopes for Allah's assistance and victory in the face of major challenges, and avoided superstitious practices and beliefs that could undermine the intelligence and good judgement of leaders. Ibn Abbas reported: *"The Messenger of Allah, peace and blessings be upon him, was optimistic and he did not see evil omens, and he liked good names".* - Musnad Ahmad

It is important that leaders develop the practice of optimism, particularly when confronting the myriads of issues that leaders often face. Lofty goals and outcomes can hardly be met without optimism and hope. Optimism helps the leader to forge ahead in the face of difficulty and seemingly insurmountable odds and inspires the group to remain hopeful and committed to the group's cause despite whatever challenges the group faces.

Having positive expectations of Allah and optimism does not mean acting without objective reasoning. Leaders must avail themselves of all information at their disposal to decide on a path forward, and then move forward deliberately and optimistically, acting on the best knowledge at their disposal. They should take a deliberative and participatory approach to leading and avail themselves of the collective wisdom of the group.

Benefits

Great outcomes can require tremendous effort to achieve and call for great determination and optimism on the part of the leader. Optimism strengthens the leader's spirit and fuels his enthusiasm for taking on the difficult task of leadership. A leader's attitude greatly influences the morale of the group he leads, and their commitment to the collective mission. Hence it is important for the leader to demonstrate faith and confidence in the path he has chosen to lead his followers on, and to encourage them with his cheerful spirit, words, and actions. This gives the followers the courage and strength to go along with the leader, particularly when the path to the desired outcome seems arduous.

Chapter 11: Understanding Balance and Relative Priorities

Managing human affairs can be complicated and understanding the relative importance and priorities of issues is a critical competency of effective leaders. One of the important duties of leaders is to make choices; choices between options that offer differing levels of benefit (or harm avoidance), and that impact those served in different ways. Leaders also have to choose between actions that are immediately impactful and those whose impact could only be felt with the passage of time. There are usually multiple forces at play that influence a leader's ultimate action and effective leadership thus calls for the leader to be able to assess the relative merits and priorities of actions, as well as to have a strong sense of balance; balance between action and inaction, change and stability, justice and mercy, steadfastness and adaptability, tradition and innovation, frugality and niggardliness, et cetera.

A corporate head might have to choose between actions that assure near-term stock performance (and the opportunity of a huge performance bonus for himself and his inner circle), and actions that ensure a more enduring long-term performance and viability of the organization with no immediate offer of reward. The same executive might also choose between actions that offer increased profitability for his organization and cause long-term damage to the environment.

Leaders need to keep in mind the relative benefits or harm of various issues or actions they consider. So, while change is important for the progress and advancement of the group, it must be introduced thoughtfully, considering the situation of the group, as well as the direct and indirect impact of such change on various stakeholders. The relative benefit of the change (as compared to the alternatives), and the opportunity cost of making the change (or of doing nothing) should be important considerations for the leader as he charts a path forward for the group.

Islam teaches moderation in all aspects of life, from the mundane acts of daily living like eating, to strict religious beliefs and rituals:

كُلُوا مِن طَيِّبَاتِ مَا رَزَقْنَاكُمْ وَلَا تَطْغَوْا فِيهِ فَيَحِلَّ عَلَيْكُمْ غَضَبِي وَمَن يَحْلِلْ عَلَيْهِ غَضَبِي فَقَدْ هَوَى

(Saying): "Eat of the good things We have provided for your sustenance, but commit no excess therein, lest My

Wrath should justly descend on you: and those on whom descends My Wrath do perish indeed! -Taha 20:81

وَالَّذِينَ إِذَا أَنفَقُوا لَمْ يُسْرِفُوا وَلَمْ يَقْتُرُوا وَكَانَ بَيْنَ ذَلِكَ قَوَامًا

Those who, when they spend, are not extravagant and not niggardly, but hold a just (balance) between those (extremes);- Al-Furqan 25:67

Islam discourages extremism in all matters, secular and religious, and Muslims are described in the Qur'an as the people of the middle way:

وَكَذَلِكَ جَعَلْنَاكُمْ أُمَّةً وَسَطًا لِّتَكُونُواْ شُهَدَاء عَلَى النَّاسِ وَيَكُونَ الرَّسُولُ عَلَيْكُمْ شَهِيدًا

And thus have We willed you to be a community of the middle way, so that [with your lives] you might bear witness to the truth before all mankind, and that the Apostle might bear witness to it before you... (Qur'an 2:143)

The Prophet (saw) said *"Beware of extremism in the religion, for that is what destroyed those before you"* - Ibn Majah. This admonition against extremism applies to all aspects of life.

The systematic approach that the Prophet (saw) took in introducing Islam to people, starting with building

Muhammad Bashir Agboola

their foundational understanding of Islam and Islamic theology of Unity of Allah (At-Tawheed) before progressing to the Islamic injunctions (dos and don'ts), is an excellent example of how to effect change amongst people. Once people have grasped the fundamental elements of a situation, it becomes easier to introduce them to more complex principles or commitments.

An important principle of Islamic teachings is the avoidance of harm to oneself and to others. The prophet (saw) said *"Do not cause harm or return harm."* - Sunan Ibn Majah. He demonstrated on multiple occasions the need to balance the potential harm of an action with the anticipated benefit, and to prioritize avoiding harm over attaining benefit when the harm outweighs the benefit in size or scope. For example, he forgo rebuilding the Kaabah (Islam's holiest site) on its original foundation for fear tearing it down to rebuild it would cause strife amongst many of the new Muslims who believed in the virtues of the Kaabah and could react unfavorably to changing it.

Also, he signed a peace treaty with the warring people of Quraysh, even though many of the terms of the treaty were considered by many Muslims at the time as disadvantageous and disrespectful to the Prophet (saw) and the Muslims. However, that peace treaty provided the Muslims enormous benefits in the ensuing decade and allowed the Muslims to practice the faith in peace,

78

and for the religion to spread widely. He recognized the longer-term and greater benefit of a peace agreement over the momentary slight and injustice the treaty represented to the Muslims.

Many Muslim communities and organizations are perennially rocked by all manners of political crisis that threaten to tear the communities apart. This is an unfortunate indication of a lack of understanding amongst the leaders and the people that the unity of the Muslim community is an obligation that must be protected, and much of the issues they squabble over are at best, matters of individual opinions or policies that have relatively little or no religious significance. They fail to realize the magnitude of the challenges they face as a community and the threat posed by the collaboration of those opposed to them. Hence this warning in the Qur'an on the imperativeness of unity of the community:

وَالَّذِينَ كَفَرُواْ بَعْضُهُمْ أَوْلِيَاء بَعْضٍ إِلاَّ تَفْعَلُوهُ تَكُن فِتْنَةٌ فِي الأَرْضِ وَفَسَادٌ كَبِيرٌ

And those who disbelieve. they are allies of one another; and unless you act likewise. there will be oppression in the world and great corruption. – Anfal 8:73

Benefits

Having a balanced outlook and understanding of the relative priorities of issues will help leaders make better informed and more effective decisions. This helps to foster unity in the community, reduces harm to the people, shows that the leader has empathy for his people, and in turn helps to build support for the leader amongst the people.

Chapter 12: Leading with Empathy

A leader can be likened to a shepherd who tends to his flock with care, watching over it, catering to its needs, protecting it against threats, and caring for its young and weak. Likewise, the leader must prioritize the well-being and protection of the people he serves. Like the shepherd does with his flock, he must watch over them, provide for their needs (by facilitating their access to the means of meeting those needs), protect the weak and needy amongst them, and guide them with gentleness and understanding.

Leading with empathy entails understanding the condition of the people, anticipating the effect of the leader and group's actions on the members, and generally treating the leader's relationship with members as one of a concerned steward with those he cares for. The leader's actions have an outsize influence over members of the group. A leader controls enormous resources of the group, corporation or state (e.g. money, military force, law or policy making power, influence, et cetera), and thus has the capacity to impact their lives significantly. His words, demeanor, and activities influence the group's sense of well-being and actual state. A leader must therefore be attuned to the effect he has on the people and behave towards them with care, understanding and empathy. He must lead with kindness and gentleness, even when his efforts seem underappreciated by the people. He should strive hard to make things easy for the people and not impose undue hardship on them.

Allah describes this leadership attitude in the relationship of the Prophet (saw) with the believers:

فَبِمَا رَحْمَةٍ مِّنَ اللهِ لِنتَ لَهُمْ وَلَوْ كُنتَ فَظًّا غَلِيظَ الْقَلْبِ لَانفَضُّواْ مِنْ حَوْلِكَ فَاعْفُ عَنْهُمْ وَاسْتَغْفِرْ لَهُمْ وَشَاوِرْهُمْ فِي الْأَمْرِ فَإِذَا عَزَمْتَ فَتَوَكَّلْ عَلَى اللهِ إِنَّ اللهَ يُحِبُّ الْمُتَوَكِّلِينَ (3:159)

It is out of Allah's mercy that you (O Prophet) have been lenient with them. Had you been cruel or hard-hearted, they would have certainly abandoned you. So, pardon them, ask Allah's forgiveness for them, and consult with them in (conducting) matters. Once you make a decision, put your trust in Allah. Surely Allah loves those who trust in Him- Al-Imran 3:159

لَقَدْ جَاءكُمْ رَسُولٌ مِّنْ أَنفُسِكُمْ عَزِيزٌ عَلَيْهِ مَا عَنِتُّمْ حَرِيصٌ عَلَيْكُم بِالْمُؤْمِنِينَ رَؤُوفٌ رَّحِيمٌ (9:128)

Now hath come unto you a Messenger from amongst yourselves: it grieves him that ye should perish: ardently anxious is he over you: to the

Believers is he most kind and merciful. – Taubah 9:128

لَا تَمُدَّنَّ عَيْنَيْكَ إِلَى مَا مَتَّعْنَا بِهِ أَزْوَاجًا مِّنْهُمْ وَلَا تَحْزَنْ عَلَيْهِمْ وَاخْفِضْ جَنَاحَكَ لِلْمُؤْمِنِينَ (15:88)

Strain not thine eyes. (Wistfully) at what We have bestowed on certain classes of them, nor grieve over them: but lower thy wing (in gentleness) to the believers. – Al- Hijr 15:88

Aisha (May Allah be pleased with her) reported: *"Whenever Allah's Apostle was given the choice of one of two matters, he would choose the easier of the two, as long as it was not sinful to do so, but if it was sinful to do so, he would not approach it. Allah's Apostle never took revenge (over anybody) for his own sake but (he did) only when Allah's Legal Bindings were outraged in which case, he would take revenge for Allah's Sake".* – Sahih Al-Bukhari.

A leader must not prefer himself over those he serves by acting in ways that benefits him to their detriment. This also ties in with the principle and practice of sincerity we discussed earlier. A leader cannot lay claim to being ethical or a person of faith when his actions are selfish and inimical to the interest of the group or stakeholders he is supposed to serve. Prophet Muhammad (saw), said: *"None of you (truly) believes, until he wishes for his brother what he wishes for himself"*. -Sahih Al-Bukhari.

Practicing empathy is critical to effective leadership, as is ensuring that others in positions of authority under the leader's oversight also lead with empathy. To ensure this happens, the leader must himself first demonstrate empathetic leadership, and enjoin it on all those he charges to manage the affairs of the group. In this regard, the leader should be both a coach and a manager, teaching this principle and holding his officials accountable for compliance. It was the practice of the prophet (saw) and the successors, to instruct and coach appointees on this and other principles of effective leadership as part of their onboarding into new leadership roles. We see this in the extensive letter Caliph Ali wrote to Malik Al-Ashtar upon appointing the latter as governor of Egypt (see appendix B), and in the advice of the prophet (saw) to Muadh Ibn Jabal when he appointed Muadh as the Governor of Yemen. The advice to Muadh as he set out to assume his post include the following snippets:

"Make things easy and do not make things difficult. Give glad tidings and do not repel people. Cooperate with each other and do not become divided." -Sahih Al-Bukhari/Sahih Muslim

"Make your character excellent for the people, O Muadh ibn Jabal."

"Be on guard from the supplication of the oppressed, for there is no barrier between it and Allah." -Sahih Al-Bukhari/Sahih Muslim

Benefits

A leader's fundamental purpose is to bring benefit to the group. Leading with empathy allows the leader to better fulfil his duties in the most humane way. A kind and considerate leader will enjoy the support of the people, benefit from their supplications for him, and avoid the evil of their resentment and invocations against him. Allah will assist the kind leader who treats his people with kindness and does right by them. Followers will reward the kind leader with their affection, loyalty, and enduring support.

Chapter 13: Practicing Self-Care

Health is wealth - thus goes a popular saying. This sentiment is shared universally, as people recognize the critical role of good health in man's ability to accomplish virtually anything worthwhile, and in his general sense of well-being.

Effective leadership can be grueling, and leaders can experience a lot of physical and mental strain and stress in the cause of their duties. Preoccupation with matters of governance can detract from the leader's capacity to care for himself and leads to the development of poor health habits that undermine the mental and physical well-being of the leader. It is thus important for the leader to consider self-care an integral requirement of effective leadership, for it is only when a leader is well that he or she can tackle the challenges of governance with the vigor and vitality it requires.

Islam emphasizes the importance of good health and wellness, with the prophet (saw) speaking of this on many occasions thus:

"Whoever among you wakes up secure in his property, healthy in his body, and he has his food for the day, it is as if he were given the entire world."- Sunan At-Tirmidhi

"There are two blessings which many people waste: health and free time." - Sahih Al-Bukhari

"You will not be given anything after the word of sincere faith like wellness, so ask Allah for wellness."- Musnad Ahmad

He thought this was important enough to teach the believers to supplicate for it*: "O Allah, grant me wellness in my body, wellness in my sight, and make my sight endure within me. There is no God but You, the Forbearing, the Generous. Glory be to Allah, the Lord of the Great Throne. All praise is due to Allah, the Lord of the worlds."* - Sunan At-Tirmidhi

The Qur'an explicitly warns against engaging in activities that are injurious to one's health and wellbeing:

$$\text{وَأَنفِقُواْ فِي سَبِيلِ اللهِ وَلاَ تُلْقُواْ بِأَيْدِيكُمْ إِلَى التَّهْلُكَةِ وَأَحْسِنُواْ إِنَّ}$$

$$\text{اللهَ يُحِبُّ الْمُحْسِنِينَ}$$

And spend of your substance in the cause of Allah, and make not your own hands contribute to (your) destruction; but do good; for Allah loveth those who do good- Al-Baqarah 2:195

Wellness involves adopting healthy habits that promote good health and wade off disease and illness. This includes practicing proper hygiene, maintaining good dietary practices, getting adequate sleep and rest, while maintaining an active lifestyle.

Hygiene

Islam describes cleanliness as a religious duty, with the prophet (saw) characterizing it as half of faith. Cleaning the body, proper grooming, oral hygiene and decent clothing are linked to many religious duties in Islam. Maintaining proper hygiene helps to stay healthy and promotes better social interaction.

Diet

Perhaps nothing influences one's health more directly than our choice of diet. What we eat and drink, when, how much, and how we do so, all play a big role in our overall health. Islam cautions against excess in anything, including eating and drinking, and has dietary rules that explicitly forbid things such as intoxicants and certain foods (including carrion and pork). While a large part of the world today suffers from hunger and poverty, there are still many areas where people overindulge and eat in excess. Many health issues are associated with overeating, which can cause obesity and associated diseases. Islam discourages gluttony and promotes moderation in eating, with Allah stating in the Qur'an:

يَا بَنِي آدَمَ خُذُوا زِينَتَكُمْ عِندَ كُلِّ مَسْجِدٍ وَكُلُوا وَاشْرَبُوا وَلَا تُسْرِفُوا ۚ إِنَّهُ لَا يُحِبُّ الْمُسْرِفِينَ

O children of Adam, take your adornment at every place of prayer. Eat and drink, but not to excess. Verily, He does not love those who commit excess. -Al-A'raf 7:31

The prophet (saw) warned against overeating, saying:
"There is no vessel which the son of Adam can fill that is more evil than his stomach, for it is enough for him to take a few bites in order to straighten his back. Yet if he is overcome by appetite, then he may fill it with a third of food, a third of drink, and a third of breath". - Sunan Ibn Majah

Fasting, when done as part of the obligatory fast in the month of Ramadhan, or as part of a voluntary fasting exercise, promotes well-documented health benefits, in addition to its spiritual effects. The health benefits include blood sugar control, reduced inflammation, and increased weight loss. Intermittent fasting, which mimics some of the same features and physiological benefits of the Islamic fasting, is now widely practiced globally as part of wellness programs and widely praised for its promotion of autophagy, which is the body's mechanism for replacing damaged cells with newer and healthier cells.

Physical Activity and Exercise

Humans are mobile beings and mobility is key to staying healthy and fit. Our bodies require moderate exercise for the continued strength of our musculoskeletal structures as well as cardiovascular health. Regular exercise is associated with reduced risk of death from a variety of ailments. Regular exercise is also linked with improved cognitive performance and is a great means of reducing the effect of mental stress. Maintaining a regular exercise schedule is a great way to stay fit but unfortunately, many leaders struggle to make the time for this. Incorporating exercise into daily activities is another way of getting some of the benefits of exercise. Examples include choosing to take the stairs over using the elevator or walking over a car ride whenever the opportunity presents itself and walking briskly as was the practice of the Prophet (saw). A brisk 20 minutes' walk 3 to 4 times a week is considered a moderate form of exercise that most people can perform. By getting out of their ivory towers and moving around their constituents (practicing *management by walking around*), leaders can both realize their exercise goals while forming more intimate relationships with those they serve. Physical exercise promotes cardiovascular health and musculoskeletal strength, and strength is favored as a quality of a believer, with the Prophet (saw) saying: *"The strong believer is more beloved to Allah than the weak believer, but there is goodness in both of them."* – Sahih Muslim

He would engage in various forms of physical activity, including on one occasion, wrestling a reputed wrestler, Rukhanah. He would also engage in racing, as Aishah reported: *"I raced with the Prophet and I beat him. Later, when I had put on some weight, we raced again, and he won. Then he said, "This cancels that (referring to the previous race)."* - Sahih Al-Bukhari. He encouraged sports such as swimming, horse riding, and archery. Many acts of worship in Islam, though spiritual, also incorporate physical activity, e.g. the rites of the holy pilgrimage (Hajj) and daily ritual prayers (salat).

Sleep and Rest

Sleep is a need of all human beings, and one without which humans cannot perform well in the short term (and will die in the mid to long term, i.e. within several days). A leader's hectic schedule often translates to very poor sleep patterns, both in terms of duration and quality. Good sleep has well documented health benefits, and inadequate sleep is linked to increased risk of death as well as higher incidence of a variety of ailments. It also reduces a person's cognitive abilities and physical vitality. Leaders need to recognize the need for sleep as an essential success factor and need to consequently manage their schedules to allow for good quality sleep nightly.

Good sleep habits include maintaining a regular sleep schedule, avoiding caffeinated beverages in the late afternoon through the evening, minimizing artificial blue lights (mostly from electronic devices) in the evening, and sleeping an adequate number of hours (generally thought to be 7 to 8 hours a day). Taking a mid-day nap (or a power nap) is well-known for its invigorating effect during the day and is the practice (sunnah) of Prophet Muhammad (saw).

Allah describes man's relationship to sleep thus:

$$\text{وَجَعَلْنَا نَوْمَكُمْ سُبَاتًا وَجَعَلْنَا اللَّيْلَ لِبَاسًا}$$

And We made your sleep for rest and the night as a covering. - An-Naba 78:9-10

A leader should manage their schedule such that they make provision for time to take breaks/rest during the day, and to get enough sleep during the night. This is considered a duty a person owes to himself, even when it comes to man's attempt to excel in religious worship.

The Prophet (saw) would often counsel those he saw pushing themselves to unhealthy extremes, as in the case of Abdullah ibn Amr, who reported:

"The Messenger of Allah, peace and blessings be upon him, said to me, 'O Abdullah, I am told you fast all day and pray all night.' I said, 'Of course, O Messenger of Allah.' The Prophet said: Do not do so. Fast and break your fast, pray in the night and sleep. Verily, your body has a right over you, your eyes have a right over you, and your wife has a right over you'."- Sahih Bukhari

Benefits

Getting adequate rest and sleep promotes good health and wellness in the leader. It staves off disease, boost performance and allows them to feel and project energy and vitality. Understanding the importance of taking an active approach to managing one's health will also influence a leader into taking actions (including official policies and resource allocation towards wellness programs) that promotes wellness in the communities they serve.

Chapter 14: Conclusion

L eadership is a trust for which the leader is accountable to those that he or she leads and, (most importantly) to God. Many qualities are essential to becoming an effective and ethical leader. However, the preceding qualities discussed in this book are some of the most important qualities observable in great leaders and advocated for in Islamic teachings.

Leaders should start out with a sincere intention to fulfil the duties of their role and should view leadership as service to the people. Leadership confers the leader with influence and often authority over the resources and affairs of the group. This power is often easy to abuse, and a leader must guard against the tendency towards this, lead with the integrity, and be as transparent as possible in their actions.

Leaders must learn to communicate effectively and should use the proven strategies of effective communications discussed in this book to increase the audience's receptivity to their message and to improve their own listening skills so they can better understand the needs of those they serve.

Justice is the bedrock of social harmony, and hence, a leader should ensure that they uphold justice within the group and deal equitably with all. In addition, a leader must work to cultivate and sustain the trust of the group as that is essential for gaining their support. Leaders should also adopt a participatory and inclusive style that leverages the collective wisdom of the group and creates in the group a sense of belonging and ownership over group affairs.

Leadership can often feel like a thankless, herculean task. It is important for the leader to maintain a positive outlook while dealing with the myriads of challenges they face. This helps to sustain the leader's spirit, as well as keep up the morale of the group.

Having to make decisions that impact the well-being of the group and the fulfilment of its objectives is one of a leader's responsibilities. Hence, the leader must learn to choose well and balance relative priorities, keeping in mind the situation and needs of the group. While doing so, the leader must also always keep the overall interest, safety, and well-being of the group at the forefront of his mind and exert himself in easing the affairs of those he serves. Serving the group with empathy is an essential practice of a good leader. The leader must serve with care, kindness, and consideration of the impact their actions can have on those in their charge.

While dealing with the stressful responsibilities of leadership, it is quite easy for the leader's own health and well-being to suffer as they become preoccupied with service to others. This could harm the leader personally and impedes their ability to lead effectively. Hence, the leader must treat self-care as an important element of being an effective leader and make time to care for their own health through appropriate health and wellness practices.

When inculcated and practiced consistently, these habits will help any leader to be effective and successful in fulfilling their leadership responsibilities and earning the favor of the group as well as divine favor, God willing.

Appendix A: Selected Ahadith/sayings of Prophet Muhammad (saw) on Leadership

Leadership Principles

"Verily, the leader is only a shield behind whom they fight, and he protects them. If he commands the fear of Allah the Exalted and justice, then he will have a reward. If he commands something else, then it will be against him." - Sahih Muslim

"When three are on a journey, they should appoint one as a leader" - Abu Dawud

"Every one of you is a shepherd and is responsible for his flock. The leader of people is a guardian and is responsible for his subjects. A man is the guardian of his family and he is responsible for them. A woman is the guardian of her husband's home and his children and she is responsible for them. The servant of a man is a guardian of the property of his master and he is responsible for it. No doubt, every one of you is a shepherd and is responsible for his flock." - Sahih Al-Bukhari/Sahih Muslim

"Whenever God makes a man responsible for other people, whether in greater or lesser numbers, he will be questioned as to whether he ruled his charges in accordance with God's decrees or not. And that will not be all. God will question him even about his family members." - Ibn Hanbal

"Woe to the rulers! Woe to the chiefs! Woe to the trustees! Some people will wish on the Day of Resurrection that their hair was hanging from the sky and swinging between heaven and earth, rather than to have done anything they did." - Musnad Ahmad

"Verily, Allah Almighty is excellent and he loves excellence." - Al-Mu'jam al-Awsat

"Verily, Allah has prescribed excellence in everything." – Sahih Muslim

"Take up good deeds only as much as you are able, for the best deeds are those done regularly even if they are few." - Sunan Ibn Majah

Just Leadership

"There are seven whom Allah will shade on a day when there is no shade but His. They are: a just ruler, a youth who grew up in the worship of Allah, one whose heart is attached to the mosques, two who love each other, meet each other, and depart from each other for the sake of Allah, a man who is tempted by a beautiful woman of high status but he rejects her, saying , 'I fear Allah,' one who spends in charity and conceals it such that his right hand does not know what his left hand has given, and one who remembered Allah in private and he wept." - Sahih Al-Bukhari/Sahih Muslim

"A day of just leadership is better than sixty years of worship, and a legal limit properly established in the land is purer for it than forty days of rain." - Al-Sunan Al-Kubra

"No one who is placed in leadership over 10 or more, then does not act justly between them, except that on the Day of Judgement he is brought in shackles and chains" – Hakim

"Verily, the most beloved of people to Allah on the Day of Resurrection and the nearest to him will be the just leader. The most hated of people to Allah and the furthest from him will be the tyrannical leader." - Sunan At-Tirmidhi

"The supplications of three are never turned back: a fasting person until he breaks his fast, a just leader, and the supplication of the oppressed is raised above the clouds by Allah, the gates of heaven open for it and the Lord says: By My might, I will surely help you in due time." - Sunan At-Tirmidhi

Leading with Integrity

"There is no governor/wali who takes charge of governing the Muslims, and then dies, and he had been cheating them, except that Allah prohibits him from Paradise" – Sahih Al-Bukhari/Sahih Muslim

"No Imam (leader) or authority spends the dark of night being deceptive in his jurisdiction, but that Allah will forbid him from entering Paradise." - Tarikh Dimashq

"No one is appointed over the affairs of the Muslims and then he does not strive for them or show them good will but that he will never enter Paradise with them."

In another narration, the Prophet (saw) said, "He does not protect them as he would protect himself and his family, but that Allah will cast him into the fire of Hell." - Al-Sunan al-Kubra

"No servant is given authority by Allah and he does not fulfill its duties sincerely but that he will never smell the fragrance of Paradise." In another narration, the

Prophet (saw) said, "Allah will forbid him from entering Paradise." - Sahih Al-Bukhari/Sahih Muslim

"Men who spend out the property of Allah without due right will go to the Fire on the Day of Judgement."- Sahih Al-Bukhari

"Those who take bribes and those who give bribes are cursed by God." - Bukhari/Muslim

"Greed and faith can never co-exist in the human heart." - An-Nasa'i

"Every traitor will have a flag on the Day of Judgement to identify them according to the amount of their treachery; there is no traitor of greater treachery than the leader of the people." – Bukhari/Muslim

"The honest and trustworthy merchant will be with the Prophets, the truthful, and the martyrs."- Sunan At-Tirmidhi

"Have integrity and make your character excellent." - Sahih Ibn Hibban

"You must be truthful. Verily, it leads to righteousness and they are both in Paradise. Beware of dishonesty, for

it leads to wickedness and they are both in the Hellfire**."**
- Al-Mu'jam Al-Kabir

"Allah said: There are three whom I will oppose on the Day of Resurrection: a man who gives his word by me but proves treacherous, a man who sells a free person into slavery and usurps his price, and a man who employs a worker and receives a completed job but he does not pay him his wages." - Sahih Al-Bukhari

Communications and Speech

"A slave (of Allah) may utter a word which pleases Allah without giving it much importance, and because of that Allah will raise him to degrees (of reward): a slave (of Allah) may utter a word (carelessly) which displeases Allah without thinking of its gravity and because of that he will be thrown into the Hell-Fire." - Sahih Al-Bukhari

"Verily, a man might speak a word to make those around him laugh, yet by it he plunges farther than the star of Pleiades." - Musnad Ahmad

"Let not fear of the people prevent one of you from speaking the truth, if he knows it."- Musnad Ahmad

"Whoever believes in Allah and the Last Day, let him speak goodness or remain silent. Whoever believes in

Allah and the Last Day, let him honor his neighbor. Whoever believes in Allah and the Last Day, let him honor his guest." – Sahih Muslim

"Do not insult anyone and do not belittle any good deed, even meeting your brother with a cheerful face or sharing your vessel with a thirsty person." - Musnad Ahmad

"Verily, I was not sent to invoke curses, but rather I was only sent as mercy." – Sahih Muslim

"Most of the sins of the children of Adam are on their tongues." - Al-Mu'jam Al-Kabir

"There is no limb on the body but that it complains of the sharpness of the tongue." - Musnad Abi Ya'la

"When the son of Adam wakes up in the morning, all of his limbs defer to the tongue and they say: Fear Allah regarding us, for we are only a part of you. If you are upright, we are upright. If you are crooked, we are crooked." - Sunan At-Tirmidhi

"Whoever restrains his tongue, Allah Almighty will cover his faults. Whoever controls his anger, Allah Almighty will protect him from His punishment.

Whoever apologizes to Allah Almighty, He will accept his apology." - Al-Ṣamt li Ibn Abi Dunya

"Whoever guards what is between his jaws and his thighs, he will enter Paradise." - Al-Mu'jam Al-Kabir

"The believer is not in the habit of cursing." - Sunan At-Tirmidhi

"The judge should not issue a ruling between two people while he is angry." - Sunan At-Tirmidhi

"It is an evil mount for a man to rely upon what others merely assert." - Sunan Abi Dawud

"If there are three of you, do not let two privately converse to the exclusion of the other."
In another narration, the Prophet said, "Do not let two privately converse to the exclusion of one, for that will hurt a believer and Allah Almighty hates for a believer to be hurt." - Sunan At-Tirmidhi

"Verily, the length of a man's prayer and the brevity of his sermon is a sign of his understanding. Lengthen the prayer and shorten the sermon. Verily, some eloquence is charming." - Sahih Muslim

Avoiding Sycophancy

"Whoever goes to the gates of the ruler will be put to trial. A servant does not move closer to the ruler but that he moves further away from Allah." - Musnad Aḥmad

Transparency

"You must be transparent and beware of secrecy." - Al-Sunnah li-Ibn Abi 'Asim

Kindness

"There is no leader who closes the door to someone in need, in hardship, and in poverty, but that Allah closes the gates of heaven to him when he is in need, in hardship, and in poverty." -Sunan At-Tirmidhi

"Verily, the worst of shepherds are the cruelest. Beware, lest you be one of them." - Sahih Muslim

"Verily, Allah did not send me to be harsh or obstinate, rather he sent me to teach and to put at ease." - Sahih Muslim

"Verily, Allah is gentle, and He loves gentleness. He grants reward for gentleness what is not given for harshness."- Sahih Ibn Hibban

"Do not cause harm or return harm. Whoever harms others, Allah will harm him. Whoever is harsh with others, Allah will be harsh with him." - Al-Sunan Al-Kubra

Positive Attitude and Optimism

"Allah Almighty says: I am as my servants expects me. If he thinks good of me, he will have it. If he thinks evil of me, he will have it." Sahih Ibn Hibban

"Verily, when Allah Almighty bestows bounties upon a servant, He loves to see the traces of His bounties upon him. He dislikes one who wallows in misery and pessimism. Allah hates the obstinate questioner, and He loves those who are modest, chaste, and sober." - Shu'ab Al-Iman

"Call upon Allah with certainty that He will answer you. Know that Allah will not answer the supplication of a heart that is unmindful and distracted." - Sunan At-Tirmidhi

"Verily, thinking well about Allah is a part of the excellent worship of Allah." - Sunan At-Tirmidhi

"When one of you supplicates, let him be determined in the supplication and he should not say: O Allah, give me if You will. There is no one to coerce Allah." – Sahih Al-Bukhari/Sahih Muslim

Advising Leaders

"Whoever intends to advise one with authority, he should not do so publicly. Rather, he should take him by the hand and advise him in private. If he accepts the advice, all is well. If he does not accept it, he has fulfilled his duty." - Musnad Aḥmad 14909

"Religion is sincere good will (advice)." We said, "To whom?" The Prophet said, "To Allah, His book, His messenger, the leaders of the Muslims, and their common people."- Sahih Muslim

Trust

"Whoever is pleased to love Allah and his messenger, or to be loved by Allah and his messenger, let him be truthful when he speaks, let him fulfill the trust to whom it is due, and let him treat well anyone who would be his neighbor."- Shu'ab al-Iman

"Fulfill the trust of those to whom they are due, and do not be treacherous to the one who betrays you."- Sunan At-Tirmidhi

"The believer is one who is trusted by people. The Muslim is one from whose tongue and hand Muslims are safe. The emigrant is one who emigrates away from evil. By the one in whose hand is my soul, a servant will not enter Paradise if his neighbor is not secure from his harm." - Sahih Ibn Hibban

"There is no faith for one who cannot be trusted. There is no religion for one who cannot keep a promise."- Musnad Aḥmad

Health and Well-Being

"There are two blessings which many people waste: health and free time." - Sahih Al-Bukhari

"Take advantage of five before five: your youth before your old age, your health before your illness, your riches before your poverty, your free time before your work, and your life before your death." - Shu'ab al-Iman

"No supplication a servant can say is better than this: O Allah, I ask You for wellness in the world and in the Hereafter." -Sunan Ibn Majah

"Ask your Lord for forgiveness and wellness in the world and the Hereafter. If you are given forgiveness and wellness in the world and the Hereafter, you have succeeded."- Sunan Ibn Majah

"Whoever among you wakes up secure in his property, healthy in his body, and he has his food for the day, it is as if he were given the entire world." - Sunan At-Tirmidhi

"There is nothing wrong with being wealthy for one who is mindful of Allah, yet good health for one who is mindful is better than wealth. And cheerfulness is among the blessings." - Sunan Ibn Majah

Gratitude

"Whoever is not grateful for small things will not be grateful for large things. Whoever does not thank people has not thanked Allah Almighty." -Al-Firdaws lil-Daylami

"Whoever is treated well, let him repay them. If he cannot find repayment, let him praise them for that is thanking them. If he conceals it, he was been ungrateful to them. Whoever adorns himself with what he has not been given, it is as if he wears a garment of lies." - Al-Adab Al-Mufrad

"I am amazed by the believer. If he is granted goodness, he praises Allah and is grateful. If he is afflicted with a calamity, he praises Allah and is patient.

The believer is rewarded for every matter, even feeding a morsel of food to his wife." - Musnad Aḥmad

Appendix B: Caliph Ali's Letter to Malik Al-Ashtar

C aliph Ali ibn Abi Talib, May Allah be pleased with him, was a beloved companion, cousin and son-in-law of Prophet Muhammad (saw), and the 4th successor (Caliph). He is noted for his piety, courage, profound wisdom, and literary prowess. His leadership example remains one of the best demonstrations of the ethical leadership principles Islam teaches. This is perhaps best illustrated in the instructions he gave to Malik Al-Ashtar. During a politically tumultuous period in the years after the passing of the Prophet (saw), Caliph Ali appointed Malik Al-Ashtar (also known as Malik Ibn Al-Harith An-Nakha'i) as the governor of Egypt in 658 CE, and wrote him a now famous letter in which he advised him on the principles of good governance.

This letter, one of the hundreds of letters, treaties, and lectures that Caliph wrote (covering topics such as religion, law, politics and philosophy), and which are now widely studied for both their intellectual arguments and literary qualities remains, almost 1400 years later, arguably one of the best manuals of the principles of ethical leadership. We have reproduced the full text of a widely available translation of the letter below.

*B*e it known to you, O, Malik, that I am sending you as Governor to a country which in the past has experienced both just and unjust rule. Men will scrutinize your actions with a searching eye, even as you used to scrutinize the actions of those before you and speak of you even as you did speak of them.

The fact is that the public speak well of only those who do good. It is they who furnish the proof of your actions. Hence the richest treasure that you may covet would be the treasure of good deeds. Keep your desires under control and deny yourself that which you have been prohibited from, for, by such abstinence alone, you will be able to distinguish between what is good to them and what is not.

Develop in your heart the feeling of love for your people and let it be the source of kindliness and blessing to them. Do not behave with them like a barbarian, and do not appropriate to yourself that which belongs to them. Remember that the citizens of the state are of two categories. They are either your brethren in religion or your brethren in kind. They are subject to infirmities and liable to commit mistakes.

Some indeed do commit mistakes. But forgive them even as you would like God to forgive you. Bear in mind that you are placed over them, even as I am placed over you. And then there is God even above him who has given you the position of a Governor in order that you may look after those under you and to be sufficient unto them. And you will be judged by what you do for them.

Do not set yourself against God, for neither do you possess the strength to shield yourself against His displeasure, nor can you place yourself outside the pale of His mercy and forgiveness. Do not feel sorry over any act of forgiveness, nor rejoice over any punishment that you may mete out to anyone. Do not rouse yourself to anger, for no good will come out of it.

Do not say: "I am your overlord and dictator, and that you should, therefore, bow to my commands", as that will corrupt your heart, weaken your faith in religion and create disorder in the state. Should you be elated by power, ever feel in your mind the slightest symptoms of pride and arrogance, then look at the power and majesty of the Divine governance of the Universe over which you have absolutely no control.

It will restore the sense of balance to your wayward intelligence and give you the sense of calmness and affability.

Beware! Never put yourself against the majesty and grandeur of God and never imitate His omnipotence; for God has brought low every rebel of God and every tyrant of man.

Let your mind respect through your actions the rights of God and the rights of man, and likewise, persuade your companions and relations to do likewise. For, otherwise, you will be doing injustice to yourself and injustice to humanity. Thus, both man and God will turn unto your enemies. There is no hearing anywhere for one who makes an enemy of God himself. He will be regarded as one at war with God until he feels contrition and seeks forgiveness. Nothing deprives man of divine blessings or excites divine wrath against him more easily than cruelty. Hence it is, that God listens to the voice of the oppressed and waylays the oppressor.

The Common Man

Maintain justice in administration and impose it on your own self and seek the consent of the people, for, the discontent of the masses sterilizes the contentment of the privileged few and the discontent of the few loses itself in the contentment of the many. Remember the privileged few will not rally round you in moments of difficulty: they will try to side-track justice, they will ask for more than what they deserve and will show no gratitude for favors done to them.

They will feel restive in the face of trials and will offer no regret for their shortcomings. It is the common man who is the strength of the State and Religion. It is he who fights the enemy. So live in close contact with the masses and be mindful of their welfare.

Keep at a distance one who peers into the weaknesses of others. After all, the masses are not free from weaknesses. It is the duty of the ruler to shield them. Do not bring to light that which is hidden, but try to remove those weaknesses which have been brought to light. God is watchful of everything that is hidden from you, and He alone will deal with it. To the best of your ability cover the weaknesses of the public, and God will cover the weaknesses in you which you are anxious to keep away from their eye.

Unloose the tangle of mutual hatred between the public and the administration and remove all those causes which may give rise to strained relations between them. Protect yourself from every such act as may not be quite correct for you. Do not make haste in seeking confirmation of tale-telling, for the taleteller is a deceitful person appearing in the garb of a friend.

The Counselors

Never take counsel of a miser, for he will vitiate your magnanimity and frighten you of poverty. Do not take the advice of a coward either, for he will weaken your resolve. Do not take counsel of the greedy: for he will instill greed in you and turn you into a tyrant. Miserliness, cowardice and greed deprive man of his trust in God.

The worst of counsellors is he who has served as a counsellor to unjust rulers and shared in their crimes. So, never let men who have been companions of tyrants or shared their crimes be your counsellors. You can get better men than these, men gifted with intelligence and foresight, but unpolluted by sin, men who have never aided a tyrant in his tyranny or a criminal in his crime. Such men will never be a burden on you. On the other hand, they will be a source of help and strength to you at all times. They will be friends to you and strangers to your enemies.

Choose such men alone for companionship both in privacy and in the public. Even among these, show preference to them who have a habitual regard for truth, however trying to you at times their truth may prove to be, and who offer you no encouragement in the display of tendencies which God does not like His friends to develop.

Keep close to you the upright, and the God fearing, and make clear to them that they are never to flatter you and never to give you credit for any good that you may not have done: for, the tolerance of flattery and unhealthy praise stimulates pride in man and makes him arrogant.

Do not treat the good and the bad alike. That will deter the good from doing good, and encourage the bad in their bad pursuits. Recompense everyone according to their deserts. Remember that mutual trust and goodwill between the ruler and the ruled are bred only through benevolence, justice and service. So, cultivate goodwill among the people; for their goodwill alone will save you from troubles. Your benevolence to them will be repaid by their trust in you, and your ill-treatment by their ill-will.

Do not disregard the noble traditions established by our forebears, which have promoted harmony and progress among the people; and do not initiate anything which might minimize their usefulness. The men who had established these noble traditions have had their reward; but responsibility will be yours if they are disturbed. Try always to learn something from the experience of the learned and wise, and frequently consult them in state matters so that you might maintain the peace and goodwill which your predecessors had established in the land.

Different Classes of People

Remember that the people are composed of different classes. The progress of one is dependent on the progress of every other, and none can afford to be independent of the other. We have the Army formed of the soldiers of God. We have our civil officers and their establishments, our judiciary, our revenue collectors and our public relations officers.

The general public itself consists of Muslims and other subjects and among them of merchants and craftsmen, the unemployed and the indigent. God has prescribed for them their rights, duties and obligations. They are all defined and preserved in the Holy Quran and in the traditions of his Prophet.

The army, by the grace of God, is like a fortress to the people and lends dignity to the state. It upholds the prestige of the faith and maintains the peace of the country. Without it the state cannot stand. In its turn, it cannot stand without the support of the state. Our soldiers have proved strong before the enemy because of the privilege God has given them to fight for Him; but they have their material needs to fulfil and have therefore to depend upon the income provided for them from the state revenue.

The military and civil population who pay revenue, both need the co-operation of others – the judiciary, civil officers and their establishment. The judge administers civil and criminal law; the civil officers collect revenue and attend to civil administration with the assistance of their establishment. And then there are the tradesmen and the merchants who add to the revenue of the state. It is they who run the markets and are in a better position than others to discharge social obligations.

Then there is the class of the poor and the needy, whose maintenance is an obligation on the other classes. God has given appropriate opportunity of service to one and all; then there are the rights of all these classes over the administration which the administrator has to meet with an eye on the good of the entire population – a duty which he cannot fulfill properly unless he takes personal interest in its execution and seeks help from God. Indeed, it is obligatory on him to impose this duty on himself and to bear with patience the inconveniences and difficulties incidental to his task.

The Army

Be particularly mindful of the welfare of those in the army who in your opinion, are staunchly faithful to their God and the prophet and loyal to their chief, and who in the hour of passion can restrain themselves and listen coolly to sensible remonstrance, and who can succor the weak and smite the strong, whom violent provocation will not throw into violent temper and who will not falter at any stage.

Keep yourself in close contact with the families of established reputation and integrity with a glorious past and draw to yourself men brave and upright in character, generous and benevolent in disposition; for such are the salt of society.

Care for them with the tenderness with which you care for your children, and do not talk before them of any good that you might have done to them, nor disregard any expression of affection which they show in return, for such conduct inspires loyalty, devotion and goodwill. Attend to every little of their wants not resting content with what general help that you might have given to them, for sometimes, timely attention to a little want of theirs brings them immense relief. Surely these people will not forget you in your own hour of need.

It behooves you to select for your Commander-in-Chief one who imposes on himself as a duty, the task of rendering help to his men, and who can excel in kindness every other officer who has to attend to the needs of the men under him, and look after their families when they are away from their homes; so much so, that the entire army should feel united in their joys and in their sorrows.

The unity of purpose will give them added strength against the enemy.

Continue to maintain a kindly attitude towards them so that they might feel attached to you. The fact is that the real happiness of the administrators and their most pleasant comfort lies in establishing justice in the state and maintaining affectionate relations with the people. Their sincerity of feeling is expressed in the love and regard they show to you, on which alone depends the safety of the administrators.

Your advice to the army will be of no avail, unless and until you show affection to both men and officers, in order that they might not regard the Government as an oppressive burden or contribute to its downfall.

Continue to satisfy their needs and praise them repeatedly for what services they have rendered. Such an attitude, God willing will inspire the brave to braver actions and induce the timid to deeds of bravery.

Try to enter into the feelings of others and do not foist the mistake of one over another and do not grudge dispensing appropriate rewards. See to it, you do not show favors to one who has done nothing but merely counts on his family position; and do not withhold proper rewards from one who has done great deeds simply because he holds a low position in life.

The Real Guidance

Turn to God and to His prophet for guidance whenever you feel uncertain as to what you have to do. There is the commandment of God delivered to those people who He wishes to guide aright:

"O people of the Faith! Obey God and obey His prophet and those from among you who hold authority over you. And refer to God and His prophet whenever there is difference of opinion among you." An-Nisa 4:59

To turn to God is in reality to consult the Book of God; and to turn to the prophet is to follow his universally accepted traditions.

Chief Justice

Select as your Chief Justice from the people, one who is by far the best among them – one who is not obsessed with domestic worries, one who cannot be intimidated, one who does not err too often, one who does not turn back from a right path once he finds it, one who is not self-centered or avaricious, one who will not decide before knowing full facts, one who will weigh with care every attendant doubt and pronounce a clear verdict after taking everything into full consideration, one who will not grow restive over the arguments of advocates and who will examine with patience every new disclosure of fact and who will be strictly impartial in his decision, one who flattery cannot mislead or one who does not exult over his position. But it is not easy to find such men.

Once you have selected the right man for the office, pay him handsomely enough, to let him live in comfort and in keeping with his position, enough to keep him above temptations. Give him a position in your court so high none can even dream of coveting it and so high that neither back-biting nor intrigue can touch him.

Subordinate Judiciary

Beware! The utmost carefulness is to be exercised in its selection: for it is this high office which adventurous self-seekers aspire to secure and exploit in their selfish interests. After the selection of your chief judge, give careful consideration to the selection of other officers.

Confirm them in their appointments after approved apprenticeship and probation. Never select men for responsible posts either out of any regard for personal connections or under any influence, for that might lead to injustice and corruption.

Of these, select for higher posts, men of experience, men firm in faith and belonging to good families. Such men will not fall an easy prey to temptations and will discharge their duties with an eye on the abiding good of others. Increase their salaries to give them a contented life.

A contented living is a help to self-purification. They will not feel the urge to tax the earnings of their subordinates for their own upkeep. They will then have no excuse either to go against your instructions or misappropriate state funds.

Keep a watch over them without their knowledge.

Perchance they may develop true honesty and true concern for the public welfare. But whenever any of them is accused of dishonesty and the guilt is confirmed by the report of your secret service, then regard this as a sufficient to convict him. Let the punishment be corporal and let that be dealt in the public at an appointed place of degradation.

Revenue Administration

Great care is to be exercised in revenue administration, to ensure the prosperity of those who pay the revenue to the state, for on their prosperity depends the prosperity of others, particularly of the masses. Indeed, the state exists on its revenue.

You should regard the proper upkeep of the land in cultivation as of greater importance than the collection of revenue, for revenue cannot be derived except by making the land productive. He who demands revenue without helping the cultivator to improve his land, inflicts unmerited hardship on the cultivator and ruins the state.

The rule of such a person does not last long. If the cultivators ask for a reduction in their land tax for having suffered from epidemics, drought, excessive rainfall, soil infertility, floods impairing the fertility of the land or the cause of crop damage, then reduce the tax accordingly, so that their condition may improve.

Do not mind the loss of revenue on that account, for that will return to you one day manifold in the hour of greater prosperity of the land and enable you to improve the condition of your towns and to raise the prestige of your state. You will be the object of universal praise. The people will believe in your sense of justice. The confidence which they will place in you in consequence will prove your strength, as they will be found ready to share your burdens.

You may settle down on the land any number of people, but discontent will overtake them if the land is not improved. The cause of the cultivator's ruin is the rulers who are bent feverishly on accumulating wealth at all costs, out of the fear that their rule might not last long. Such are the people who do not learn from examples or precedents.

Clerical Establishment

Keep an eye on your establishment and on your scribes, select the best among them for your confidential correspondence such among these, as possess high character and deserve your full confidence, men who may not exploit their privileged position to go against you, who may not grow neglectful of their duties, who in the drafting of treaties may not succumb to external temptation and harm your interests, or fail to render you proper assistance and to save you from trouble, who in carrying out their duties can realize their serious responsibilities, for he who does not realize his own responsibilities can hardly appraise the responsibilities of others.

Do not select men for such work merely on the strength of your first impressions of your affection or good faith, for as a matter of fact, the pretensions of a good many who are really devoid of honesty and good breeding, may cheat even the intelligence of rulers. Selection should be made after due probation, which should be the test of righteousness.

In making direct appointments from people, see to it that those selected possess influence with the people and who enjoy the reputation of being honest, for such selection is agreeable to God and the ruler. For every department of administration, let there be a head, whom no trying task might cause worry and no pressure of work annoy.

Remember, every weakness of any one among your establishment and scribes, which you may overlook, will be written down against you in your scroll of deeds.

Trade and Industry

Treat businessmen and artisans well and advise others to do likewise. Some of them live in towns, while some move from place to place with their wares and tools earning their living by manual labor. Trade and industry are the real sources of profit to the state and the suppliers of consumer goods.

While the general public is not inclined to bear the strain, those engaged in these professions take the trouble to collect commodities from far and near, from land and across the sea, from mountains and forests and naturally derive benefits.

It is this class of peace-loving people from whom no disturbance need be feared. They love peace and order; indeed, they are incapable of creating disorder. Visit every part of the country and establish personal contact with this class and inquire into their condition.

But bear in mind that a good many of them are intensely greedy and are inured to bad dealings. They hoard grain and try to sell it at a high price, and this is most harmful to the public. It is a blot on the name of the ruler not to fight this evil. Prevent them from hoarding, for the prophet of God had prohibited it.

See to it, that trade is carried on with the utmost ease, that the scales are evenly held and that prices are so fixed that neither the seller nor the buyer is put to a loss. If despite your warning, anyone should go against your commands and commit the crime of hoarding, then deal him appropriately with a severe punishment.

The Poor

Beware! Fear God when dealing with the problem of the poor who have none to patronize them, who are forlorn, indigent, helpless and are greatly torn in mind – victims of the vicissitudes of time. Among them are some who do not question their lot in life and who, notwithstanding their misery, do not go about seeking alms.

For God's sake, safeguard their rights, for on you rests the responsibility of protecting their interests.

Assign for their uplift a portion of the state exchequer (Bayt al-Mal), wherever they may be, whether close at hand or far away from you. The rights of the two should be equal in your eye. Do not let any preoccupation slip *them from your mind, for no excuse whatsoever for the disregard of their rights will be acceptable to God.*

Do not treat their interests as of less importance than your own, and never keep them outside the purview of your important considerations and mark the persons who look down upon them and of whose conditions they keep you in ignorance.

Select from among your officers such men as are meek and God fearing who can keep you properly informed of the condition of the poor. Make such provision for these poor people as shall not oblige you to offer an excuse before God on the Day of Judgement for, it is this section of the people which, more than any other, deserves benevolent treatment.

Seek your reward from God by giving to each of them what is due to him and enjoin on yourself as a sacred duty the task of meeting the needs of such aged among them as have no independent means of livelihood and are averse to seek alms. The discharge of this duty is what usually proves very trying to rulers but is very welcome to societies which are gifted with foresight. It is only such societies or nations who truly carry out with equanimity their covenant with God to discharge their duty to the poor.

Open Conferences

Meet the oppressed and the lowly periodically in an open conference and conscious of the divine presence there, have a heart-to-heart talk with them, and let none from your armed guard or civil officers or members of the Police or the Intelligence Department be by your side, so that the representatives of the poor might state their grievances fearlessly and without reserve.

For I have heard the prophet of God say that no nation or society, in which the strong do not discharge their duty to the weak, will occupy a high position.

Bear with composure any strong language which they may use, and do not get annoyed if they cannot state their case lucidly. Even so, God will open for you his door of blessings and rewards. Whatever you can give to them, give it ungrudgingly and whatever you cannot afford to give, make that clear to them in utmost sincerity.

There are certain things which call for prompt action. One of them is correspondence regarding the redress of grievances, which your heedless staff have been unable to tackle. See to it that petitions or applications that are submitted for your consideration, are brought to your notice without any delay, however much your officers might try to intercede them. Dispose of the day's work that very day, for the coming day will bring with it its own tasks.

Communion with God

Do not forget to set apart the best of your time for communion with God, although every moment of yours is for Him only, provided it is spent sincerely in the service of your people. The special time that you give to prayer, is to be devoted to the performances of the prescribed daily prayers. Keep yourself engaged in these prayers both in the day and in the night, and to gain perfect communion, do not as far as possible, let your prayers grow tiresome.

When you lead in congregational prayer, do not let your prayer be so lengthy as to cause discomfort to the congregation or raise in them the feeling of dislike for it or liquidate its effect, for in the congregation there may be invalids and also those who have to attend pressing affairs of their own.

When, on receiving an order to proceed to Yemen, I asked of the prophet of God, how I should lead the people there in prayer, he said "Perform your prayers even as the weakest among you would do, and set an example of consideration to the faithful".

Aloofness Is Undesirable

Alongside the observance of all that I have said, bear one thing in mind. Never, for any length of time, keep yourself aloof from the people, for to do so is to keep oneself ignorant of their affairs. It develops in the ruler a wrong perspective and renders him unable to distinguish between what is important and what is not, between right and wrong, and between truth and falsehood. The ruler is after all human, and he cannot form a correct view of anything which is out of sight.

There is no distinctive sign attached to truth which may enable one to distinguish between the different varieties of truth and falsehood. The fact is that you must be one of two things. Either you are just or unjust. If you are just, then you will not keep yourself away from the people but will listen to them and meet their requirements. But, if you are unjust, the people themselves will keep way from you.

What virtue is there in your keeping aloof? At all events aloofness is not desirable, especially when it is your duty to attend to the needs of the people. Complaints of oppression by your officers or petitions for justice should not prove irksome to you.

Make this clear to yourself that those immediately about and around you, will like to exploit their position to covet what belongs to others and commit acts of injustice. Suppress such a tendency in them.

Make a rule of your conduct never to give even a small piece of land to any of your relations. That will prevent them from causing harm to the interests of others and save you from courting the disapprobation of both God and man.

Deal justice squarely, regardless of whether one is a relation or not. If any of your relations or companions violates the law, mete out the punishment prescribed by law, however painful it might be to you personally, for it will be all to the good of the state. If at any time people suspect, that you have been unjust to them in any respect, disclose your mind to them and remove their suspicions. In this way, your mind will get attuned to the sense of justice and people will begin to love you. It will also fulfill your wish that you should enjoy their confidence.

Peace and Treaties

Bear in mind that you do not throw away the offer of peace which your enemy may himself make. Accept it, for that will please God. Peace is a source of comfort to the army; it reduces your worries and promotes order in the state.

But Beware! Be on your guard when the peace is signed for, certain types of enemies propose terms of peace just to lull you into a sense of security only to attack you again when you are off your guard. So, you should exercise the utmost vigilance on your part, and place no undue faith in their protestations.

But, if under the peace treaty you have accepted any obligations, discharge those obligations scrupulously. It is a trust and must be faithfully upheld and whenever you have promised anything, keep it with all the strength that you command, for whatever differences of opinion might exist on other matters, there is nothing so noble as the fulfilment of a promise.

This is recognized even among non-Muslims, for they know the dire consequences which follow from the breaking of covenants. So never make excuses in discharging your responsibilities and never break a promise, nor cheat your enemy. For breach of promise is an act against God, and none except the positively wicked acts against God.

Indeed, Divine promises are a blessing spread over all mankind. The promise of God is a refuge sought after, even by the most powerful on earth, for there is no risk of being cheated. So, do not make any promise from which you may afterwards offer excuses to retract, nor go back upon what you have confirmed to abide by, nor break it, however galling it may at first prove to be. For it is far better to wait in patience for wholesome results to follow, than to break it out of any apprehensions.

Beware! Abstain from shedding blood without a valid cause. There is nothing more harmful than this which brings about one's ruin. The blood that is willfully shed shortens the life of a state. On the Day of Judgement, it is this crime for which one will have to answer first. So, beware! Do not wish to build the strength of your state on blood for, it is this blood which ultimately weakens the state and passes it into other hands. Before me and my God no excuse for willful killing can be entertained.

Murder is a crime which is punishable by death. If on any account the corporal punishment dealt by the state for any lesser crime results in the death of the guilty, let not the prestige of the state stand in any way of the deceased relations claiming compensation.

Final Instructions

Do not make haste to do a thing before its time, nor put it off when the right moment arrives. Do not insist on doing a wrong thing, nor show slackness in rectifying a wrong thing. Perform everything in its proper time and let everything occupy its proper place.

When the people as a whole agree upon a thing, do not impose your own will on them and do not neglect to discharge the responsibility that rests on you in consequence. For, the eyes of the people will be on you and you are answerable for whatever you do to them. The slightest dereliction of duty will bring its own retribution.

Keep your anger under control and keep your hands and tongue in check. Whenever you fall into anger, try to restrain yourself or else you will simply increase your worries.

It is imperative on you to study carefully the principles which have inspired just and good rulers who have gone before you. Give close thought to the example of our prophet, his traditions, and the commandments of the Holy Qur'an and whatever you might have assimilated from my own way of dealing with things.

Endeavour to the best of your ability to carry out the instructions which I have given you here and which you have solemnly undertaken to follow. By means of this order, I enjoin on you not to succumb to the prompting of your own heart or to turn away from the discharge of duties entrusted to you.

I seek the refuge of the might of the Almighty and of His limitless sphere of blessings, and invite you to pray with me that He may give us together the grace willingly to surrender our will to His will, and to enable us to acquit ourselves before Him and His creation, so that mankind might cherish our memory and our work survive.

I seek of God the culmination of his blessings and pray that He may grant you and me His grace and the honor of martyrdom in His cause. Verily, we have to return to Him. I invoke His blessings on the Prophet of God and his pure progeny.

About the Author

Muhammad Bashir Agboola is an Islamic activist, community leader and senior-level executive with several years of management and leadership experience in top-tier corporations in the United States. He has served in various capacities with a number of professional and Islamic organizations, including as a member of the Board of Directors of the Islamic Education Foundation of New Jersey, the Imams Council of Newark, New Jersey, and the Mission Board of Masjid Mubarak (NAIM), Newark, New Jersey, United State.

He writes and speaks on a variety of professional and Islamic topics.

He holds multiple professional and academic certifications and credentials including a Master degree in Computer Science and an MBA in Finance.

Works Cited

Ahmad. (n.d.). *Musnad Ahmad*. Retrieved from Daily Hadith
Online: https://abuaminaelias.com/dailyhadithonline/

Al-Bukhari. (n.d.). *Sahih Al-Bukhari*. Retrieved from Daily Hadith
Online: https://abuaminaelias.com/dailyhadithonline/

Ali. (n.d.). *Caliph Ali's Letter to Malik Al-Ashtar*. Retrieved from
https://www.al-islam.org/richest-treasure-imam-
ali/imam-ali-s-letter-malik-al-ashtar-richest-treasure

Al-Iman. (n.d.). *Shu'ab Al-Iman*. Retrieved from Daily Hadith
Online: https://abuaminaelias.com/dailyhadithonline/

Al-Kubra. (n.d.). *Al-Sunan Al-Kubra*. Retrieved from Daily Hadith
Online: https://abuaminaelias.com/dailyhadithonline/

An-Nasa'i. (n.d.). *An-Nasa'i*. Retrieved from Daily Hadith Online:
https://abuaminaelias.com/dailyhadithonline/

At-Tirmidhi. (n.d.). *Sunan At-Tirdmidhi*. Retrieved from Daily
Hadith   Online:
https://abuaminaelias.com/dailyhadithonline/

Greenleaf, R. K. (2002). *Servant Leadership.* Mahwah, New Jersey:
Paulist Press.

Hesse, H. (n.d.). *Journey to the East.* Mansfield Centre, CT: Martino
Publishing.

Ibn-Abī'Āṣim. (n.d.). *Al-Sunnah li-Ibn Abī 'Āṣim*. Retrieved from
Daily   Hadith   Online:
https://abuaminaelias.com/dailyhadithonline/

IbnHibban. (n.d.). *Sahih Ibn Hibban*. Retrieved from Daily Hadith
Online: https://abuaminaelias.com/dailyhadithonline/

Majah, I. (n.d.). *Ibn Majah*. Retrieved from Daily Hadith Online:
https://abuaminaelias.com/dailyhadithonline/

Muslim. (n.d.). *Sahih Muslim*. Retrieved from Daily Hadith Online:
    https://abuaminaelias.com/dailyhadithonline/
Qur'an. (n.d.). *Translation of the Meaning of the Qur'an*. Retrieved
    from Islamic City: https://www.islamicity.org/quran/

Index

Made in the USA
Coppell, TX
03 January 2022

70716050R00090